LIFE-CHANGING CHRISTIAN CLASSICS

Christian Book Sampler 2

What Goes Into the Mind™
Comes Out in a Life

CBA
Colorado Springs, Colorado

Life-Changing Christian Classics
Christian Book Sampler 2
© 2004 by Christian Booksellers Association (CBA)

Summer 2004 Edition
Published by CBA
9240 Explorer Drive, Colorado Springs, CO 80920

Profits from the *Life-Changing Christian Classics* will be used
to support the distribution of Christian resources outside the United States.

Printed in the United States of America
by Bethany Press Intl., Bloomington, MN

Table of Contents

Foreword

My interest in apologetics (the defense of Christianity) began back in college when I was challenged by several students to examine the claims of Jesus Christ. After much study, I could only come to one conclusion: Jesus Christ is the Son of God, He was crucified, He died, He was resurrected on the third day, and offered me a transformed relationship with Him. I committed my life to Christ, and He did in fact change my life.

As one who had set out to prove Christianity false, I have had a unique opportunity to proclaim the Truth of Jesus Christ. Over the past 39 years, God has given me many opportunities to speak at college campuses and churches worldwide. He also has led me to author many books on apologetics—including two that are included in this sampler.

As I look back over these many years of blessing and ministry, I realize anew the impact Christian books have had in my life. Not only does a great deal of the information I use to monitor our changing culture come from published research, but I also equally rely on the classic books written many years ago.

And that's why I am happy to write this foreword. You and I both have a great deal to learn from those who have gone before. These saints have experienced this precious faith from a

different perspective, living in a culture quite
different from ours today. But, their insightful
messages still apply to our lives.

I encourage you to listen and learn from
Andrew Murray and A.W. Tozer and Watchman
Nee and others whose books are featured in this
sampler. Their messages are timeless and powerful and will stimulate you in your walk with God.

Josh McDowell

*I keep asking that the God of our Lord Jesus Christ, the glorious
Father, may give you the Spirit of wisdom and revelation, so that
you may know him better. I pray also that the eyes of your heart
may be enlightened in order that you may know the hope to which
he has called you, the riches of his glorious inheritance in the saints.*
(Ephesians I: 17, 18 NIV)

Introduction

How does Christian literature become "classic"? Does who the author is determine the book's status? Is it the age of the work? Or the subject matter?

We'd like to suggest these books endure because they provide solid answers to the spiritual questions that arise age after age.

You may not know the writings of Amy Carmichael, Brother Lawrence, or Richard Foster—or believe they can apply to your busy daily life. However, are the topics of praising God, prayer, living a spirit-filled life, and apologetics only limited to a time long ago?

In this volume, you'll find works dated from the 1600s to as recently as a few years ago. They are classics because they have—and will—stand the test of time.

You'll also notice in this book the phrase "What Goes Into the Mind Comes Out in a Life."™ It's a reminder that whatever you read, watch on television or listen to on the radio will impact your life. Will the results be positive or negative? As you turn the pages to these classic readings, we know it will be positive.

We hope you enjoy this free sampler. Be sure to return to your local Christian store with the coupons provided at the back of the book, and buy a title or two for yourself or a friend. While you're there, browse the fine music selection. Check out the inspirational gift product. Your local Christian store is a source for product that will indeed put good things into your mind.

Turn the page and begin a journey into the wonderful world of classic Christian literature.

The Publisher

The publisher wishes to thank Bethany Press International for printing services and generous support of this project, Lora Riley for editorial services, and Jackie Kludt for cover and graphic design. A special thanks is due to the Christian publishers who supported this sampler by placing titles and to the Christian booksellers for their commitment to impact their communities for Christ by distributing this collection of life-changing titles.

∽ HISTORICAL FICTION ∾
Love Comes Softly
JANETTE OKE

*Clark and Marty Davis'
"marriage of convenience"
turns into true and
abiding love in this tale
of loss, growing faith,
and hope.*

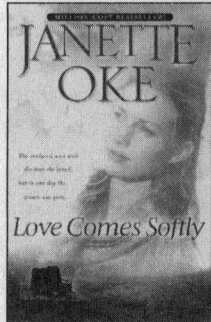

THE MORNING SUN SHONE brightly on the canvas
of the covered wagon, promising an unseasonably
warm day for mid-October. Marty fought for
wakefulness, coming slowly out of a troubled and
fitful sleep. Why did she feel so heavy and ill at
ease—she who usually woke with enthusiasm and
readiness for each new day's adventure? Then it all
came flooding back, and she fell in a heap on the

quilt from which she had just emerged. Sobs shook her body, and she pressed the covering to her face to muffle the sound.

Clem is gone. The truth of it was nearly unthinkable. Less than two short years ago, strong, adventurous, boyish Clem had quickly and easily made her love him. Self-assured and confident, he had captured her heart and her hand. Fourteen months later, she was a married woman out west, beginning a new and challenging adventure with the man she loved—until yesterday.

Oh, Clem, she wept. Her whole world had fallen around her when the men came to tell her that Clem was dead. Killed outright. His horse had fallen. They'd had to destroy the horse. Did she want to come with them?

No, she'd stay.

Would she like the missus to come over?

No, she'd manage.

She wondered how she had even gotten the words past her lips.

They'd care for the body, one of them had told her. His missus was right good at that. The neighbors would arrange for the burying. Lucky the parson was paying his visit through the area. Was to have moved on today, but they were certain that he'd stay over. Sure she didn't want to come with them?

No, she'd be all right.

Hated to leave her alone.

She needed to be alone.

They'd see her on the morrow. Not to worry. They'd care for everything.

Thank ya—

And they had gone, taking her Clem with them, wrapped in one of her few blankets and fastened on the back of a horse. The kindly neighbor should have been riding it, but he was now leading the animal slowly, careful of its burden.

And now it was the morrow and the sun was shining. Why was the sun shining? Didn't nature know that today should be as lifeless as she felt, with a cold wind blowing like the chill that gripped her heart?

The fact that she was way out west in the fall of the year with no way back home, no one around that she knew—and she was expecting Clem's baby besides—should have filled her with panic. But for the moment the only thing her mind could settle on and her heart grasp was the overwhelming pain of her great loss.

"Oh, Clem! Clem!" she cried aloud. "What am I gonna do without you?" She buried her face again in the quilt.

Clem had come out west with such wild excitement.

"We'll find everything we want there in thet new country. The land's there fer the takin'," he had exulted.

"What 'bout the wild animals—an' the Injuns?" she had stammered.

He had laughed at her silliness, picked her up
in his strong arms, and whirled her around in the air.

"What 'bout a house? It'll be 'most winter
when we git there," she worried.

"The neighbors will help us build one. I've
heered all 'bout it. They'll help one another do
whatever needs to be done out there."

And it was true. Those hardy frontiersmen
scattered across the wilderness would leave their
highly valued crops standing in the fields, if need
be, while they gave of their time to put a roof over a
needy if somewhat cocky and reckless newcomer,
because they would know far better than he the
fierceness of the winter winds.

"We'll make out jest fine. Don't ya worry
yourself none, Marty," Clem had assured her. With
some reluctance, Marty had begun preparations for
the long trek by wagon train to follow her beloved
husband's dream.

After many weeks of travel, they had come
upon a farmhouse in an area of rolling hills and
pastureland, and Clem had made inquiries. Over a
friendly cup of coffee, the farmer had informed
them that he owned the land down to the creek, but
the land beyond that, reaching up into the hills, had
not yet been claimed. With an effort, Clem had
restrained himself from whooping on the spot.
Marty could tell that the very thought of being so
near his dream filled Clem with wild anticipation.
Thanking their soon-to-be neighbor, they hurried

on, traveling a bit too fast for the much-mended wagon. They were within sight of their destination when another wheel gave way, and this time it was beyond repair.

They had camped for the night, still on the neighbor's land, and Clem had piled rocks and timbers under the broken wagon in an effort to make it somewhat level. In the morning they had discovered more bad luck. One of the horses had deserted them during the night, and his broken rope still dangled from the tree. Clem had ridden out on the remaining horse to look for it. And then the accident, and now he wouldn't be coming back. There would be no land claimed in his name, nor a house built that would stand proud and strong to shelter his wife and baby.

Marty sobbed again, but then she heard a noise outside the wagon and peeped timidly through the canvas. Neighbors were there—four men with grim faces, silently and soberly digging beneath the largest spruce tree. As she realized what their digging meant, a fresh torment tore at her soul. *Clem's grave.* It was really true. This horrible nightmare was actually happening. Clem was gone. She was without him. He would be buried on borrowed land.

"Oh, Clem. What'll I do?"

She wept until she had no more tears. The digging continued. She could hear the scraping of the shovels, and each thrust seemed to stab deeper into her heart.

More sounds reached her, and she realized
that other neighbors were arriving. She must take
herself in hand. Clem would not want her hiding
away inside the wagon.

She climbed from the quilt and tried to tidy
her unruly hair. Quickly dressing in her dark blue
cotton frock, which seemed to be the most suitable
for the occasion, she snatched a towel and her comb
and slipped out of the wagon and down to the
spring to wash away her tears and straighten her
tangled hair. This done, she squared her shoulders,
lifted her chin, and went back to meet the somber
little group gathered under the spruce.

It was hot in there at midday, and the rush of
torrid air sent her already dizzy head to spinning.
She crawled back out and down on the grass on the
shady side of the wagon, propping herself up against
the broken wheel. Her senses seemed to be playing
tricks on her. Round and round in her head swept
the whirlwind of grief, making her wonder what
truly was real and what imagined. She was mentally
groping to make some sense of it all when a male
voice suddenly made her jump with its closeness.

"Ma'am."

She lifted her head and looked up. A man
stood before her, cap in hand, fingering it deter-
minedly as he cleared his throat. She vaguely
recognized him as one of the shovel bearers. His

height and build evidenced strength, and there was an oldness about his eyes that belied his youthful features. Her eyes looked into his face, but her lips refused to respond.

He seemed to draw courage from somewhere deep inside himself and spoke again.

"Ma'am, I know thet this be untimely—ya jest havin' buried yer husband an' all. But I'm afraid the matter can't wait none fer a proper-like time an' place."

He cleared his throat again and glanced up from the hat in his hands.

"My name be Clark Davis," he hurried on, "an' it 'pears to me thet you an' me be in need of one another."

A sharp intake of breath from Marty made him pause, then raise a hand.

"Now, hold a minute," he told her, almost a command. "It jest be a matter of common sense. Ya lost yer man an' are here alone." He cast a glance at the broken wagon wheel, then crouched down to speak directly to her.

"I reckon ya got no money to go to yer folks, iffen ya have folks to go back to. An' even if thet could be, ain't no wagon train fer the East will go through here 'til next spring. Me, now, I got me a need, too."

He stopped there and his eyes dropped. It was a minute before he raised them and looked into her face. "I have a little 'un, not much more'n a mite—

an' she be needin' a mama. Now, as I see it, if we marries, you an' me"—he looked away a moment, then faced her again—"we could solve both of those problems. I would've waited, but the preacher is only here fer today an' won't be back through agin 'til next April or May, so's it has to be today."

He must have recognized in her face the sheer horror Marty was feeling.

"I know. I know," he stammered. "It don't seem likely, but what else be there?"

What else indeed? raged through Marty's brain. *I'd die first, that's all. I'd rather die than marry you—or any man. Get out. Go away.*

But he didn't read any more of her rampaging thoughts and went on. "I've been strugglin' along, tryin' to be pa an' ma both fer Missie, an' not doin' much of a job of it, either, with tryin' to work the land an' all. I've got me a good piece of land an' a cabin thet's right comfortable like, even if it be small, an' I could offer ya all the things thet a woman be a needin' in exchange fer ya takin' on my Missie. I be sure thet ya could learn to love her. She be a right pert little thing." He paused. "But she do be needin' a woman's hand, my Missie. That's all I be askin' ya, ma'am. Jest to be Missie's mama. Nothin' more. You an' Missie can share the bedroom. I'll take me the lean-to. An' ..." He hesitated a bit. "I'll promise ya this, too. When the next wagon train goes through headin' east to where ya can catch yerself a stagecoach, iffen ya ain't happy here, I'll see to yer fare back home—on one condition—thet ya take my Missie along with ya." He paused to swallow, then said, "It jest don't be fair to the little mite not to have a mama."

He rose suddenly. "I'll leave ya to be a thinkin' on it, ma'am. We don't have much time."

He turned and strode away. The sag of his shoulders told her how much the words had cost him. Still, she thought angrily, what kind of a man could propose marriage—even this kind of a marriage—to a woman who had just turned from her husband's grave? She felt despair well up within her. *I'd rather die,* she told herself. *I'd rather die.* But what of Clem's baby? She didn't want death for their little one, neither for her sake nor for Clem's. Frustration and anger and grief whirled through her. What a situation to be in. No one, nothing, out in this Godforsaken country. Family and friends were out of reach, and she was completely alone. She knew he was right. She needed him, and she hated him for it.

"I hate this country! I hate it! I hate him, the cold, miserable man! I hate him! I hate him!" But even as she stormed against him, she knew she had no way around it.

She wiped her tears and got up from the shady grass. She wouldn't wait for him to come back in his lordly fashion for her decision, she thought stubbornly, and she went into the wagon and began to pack the few things she called hers.

WITH PROFOUND SIMPLICITY, JANETTE OKE writes of what she
knows best—real life, honest love, and lasting values. With
more than 75 titles and 22 million in sales, her stories tran-
scend time and place. Readers of all ages identify with the
everyday events and emotions of her characters. Her writing
has received many honors, including the 1992 ECPA
President's Award for her significant contribution to
Christian fiction and the 1999 CBA Life Impact Award.

LOVE COMES SOFTLY
Paper, 237 pages
© 1979, 2003 by Janette Oke
Bethany House Publishers
ISBN: 0764228323

〜 INSPIRATIONAL 〜

Come Away My Beloved

FRANCES J. ROBERTS

Meet your loving heavenly Father in this evocative devotional. For more than 30 years, it's moved believers to live more fully for a holy Savior.

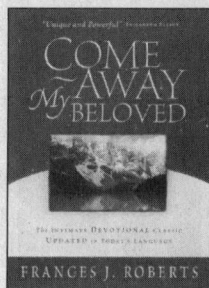

"Eye has not seen, nor ear heard, Nor have entered into the heart of man the things which God has prepared for those who love Him."
(1 Cor. 2:9)

YOU HAVE READ THAT "the letter kills, but the Spirit gives life" (2 Cor. 3:6). I have a deeper revelation of this truth to give you if you can receive it. For the

Spirit operates in a different realm than the Word. The Word deals with you on the plane of your everyday living. It governs your conduct in daily affairs. It guides you into the knowledge of the doctrines of God, the understanding of My divine will, and instructs you in the walk of the Christian.

But in the Spirit, there is a life awaiting that would draw you out beyond the confines of the natural world. The Spirit of God operates in the realm of the supernatural and the infinite.

Do not hold back in wonder and disbelief. Accept My life in the Spirit as it is. Do not require Me to operate within the limitations of your life. I am calling you to give My Spirit within you the liberty to move out into the dimensions of the infinite.

Breathtaking? Perhaps. But how could you expect anything less of Me? Push open the door. In the dazzling light of My presence you will see much that is now obscure to you because you have chosen to walk in the darkness. I have better things for you—things in keeping with Myself. You have not truly known Me. You have been hindered in your comprehension by what you have read and been taught. There is very little more concerning Me that you can learn from human sources. You can know Me in the Spirit only when you go deeper in your worship. I am not found in textbooks but in sanctuaries. You are not changed by knowledge but by love. Only the heart that is melted in devotion is pliable in My hand. Only the mind that is open to the Spirit can receive divine revelation.

Labor not to be wise but to be yielded, and in your attitude of submission to My Spirit I will instruct you in My truth. There will be death and there will be a glorious resurrection. The letter will convict of sin and prune away the old fallen nature, and the Spirit will bring forth within you a life that will never die. It will have faculties of perception not to be compared with the physical senses, for the mind of the Spirit is the Mind of Christ.

It shall increase and develop as you move on into God, and you will leave behind religious intellectualism and discover a more glorious way.

The Secret of Silence
(Praise and Reproof)

> Behold, you are fair, my love!
> Behold, you are fair!
> (Song of Solomon 1:15)

My child, do not let the words of others influence you unduly—neither their praise nor their criticism. Weigh each for its proper value, and come back to Me again. Only in communion with Me can you be sure of the truth. If I correct you, you know it is for your betterment. If I encourage you with a word of praise, it is because I know you need it; so rejoice in it and accept it as wholeheartedly as you accept My rebukes.

You know My rebukes are for your benefit. Can you not believe that My words of commendation are for the same purpose? Some of your faults and weaknesses can best be helped and corrected by praise rather than by reproof. When you turn a deaf ear in an effort to be humble, you are not helping. You cannot be truly humble until you have a deep sense of being loved.

Knowing and truly feeling that such great love is not merited in the face of your many imperfections will generate more honest humility than a thousand rebukes for obvious failures. You are condemned already by your own heart. There is a subtle pride that seeks to hide these glaring imperfections in the effort to hold some vestige of self-esteem and invoke the respect of others. This is a craftiness of the enemy.

If you will accept My love and My approval, you will be given courage to face your sins and faults so you can deal with them more decisively. The more you find of the truth about your own self, the more you will be set free . . . free from improper evaluations of your worth, free from false pride that seeks to cover recognized flaws.

I want your life, character, and personality to be as beautiful and lovely as I visualized you to be when I created you. Much has not developed perfectly. Some early beauty has been marred. Live close to Me, and let Me remold and re-create until

I see in you the image of all I want you to be.

I love you, My child—My very dear and special child. Through your childhood years I walked very close to you, and in your child-like way you were very conscious of My presence and reality. You have made an arduous journey. You have climbed many mountains that you could easily have walked around. You have not chosen the pleasant path nor sought joys though they were readily accessible.

You have often misconstrued My will and felt that only in sacrifice and suffering could you please Me, while much of the time I have longed to deliver you out of the very pains you inflicted upon yourself. You meant to please Me, but in truth you were only marring your own beauty which is precious to Me.

I cannot rejoice in a blighted rose. You have gone far enough in this way. I offer you My path now, if you are strong enough to accept it. Life, liberty, love, and joy. Health and peace—simplicity and rest. It has been there for you all along. You can have it even now if you will.

I do not want you to work for Me under pressure and tension like a machine—striving to produce, produce. I only want you to live with Me as a person. I have waited for you to wear yourself out. I knew you would find it eventually—the secret of silence and rest, of solitude and song.

I will rebuild your strength—not to work again in foolish frenzy, but just for the sake of making you strong and well. To Me this is an end in itself. Make it your aim and join with Me wholeheartedly in the project. Many joys are waiting yet.

The Love Covenant

> All the paths of the Lord are mercy and truth,
>> To such as keep His covenant.
>>> (Psalm 25:10)

My children, there is no good thing that I would withhold from you. I have not left you to fend for yourselves nor to make your way by your own devices. I am the Lord your God. I am your provider and your defender. I care for you with a deep and tender love. I am all-wise and all-powerful and will be your defense against every onslaught of the enemy.

Anticipate My help. I will not fail you. Look down at the path before you. You will see the print of My feet. "'I will go before you and make the crooked places straight'" (Isaiah 45:2). I will make the path ready for you as you follow.

It is a joy to My heart when My children rely on Me. I delight in working things out for you, but I delight even more in you yourself than in anything I do to help you. Even so, I want you to delight in Me just for Myself, rather than in anything you do for Me.

Service is the salvage of love. It is like the

twelve baskets of bread that were left over. The bread that was eaten was like fellowship mutually given; and the excess and overflow was a symbol of service. I do not expect you to give to others until you have first eaten. I will provide you with plentiful supply to give if you first come to receive for your own needs.

This is not selfishness. It is the Law of Life. Can the stalk of corn produce the ear unless first it receives its own life from the parent seed? No more can you produce fruit in your ministry unless you are impregnated with divine life from its source in God Himself. It was from the hands of the Christ that the multitudes received bread. From His hands you also must receive your nurture, the Bread of Life to sustain your health and your life.

This is His love-covenant with you. It is the message of John 15:4: "'Abide in Me, and I in you. As the branch cannot bear fruit of itself, unless it abides in the vine, neither can you, unless you abide in Me.'" This abiding is a love relationship, and this is why service is the salvage of love.

Service will be futile and burdensome unless it springs from an overflowing heart. Overflowing not with good intentions and condescending self-righteousness, but overflowing with the love of God. This you do not have of yourself, nor can you give, however much you might desire to do so. You will possess this love only as you wait upon Me and take time to absorb it from Me, like a quiet flower takes life from the warm rays of the sun.

Your heart will be cold otherwise. For your ready ardor and natural sympathy, and common kindness will soon be cooled by the chill winds of ingratitude and others' unlovely reactions. Do you think the love of Jesus was always well received? Would He not have brought His ministry to an abrupt end on many an occasion if He had needed the appreciation of people to motivate His loving service?

Have you read the reaction of the religious people to the recital of His miracle-working power in Luke 4? The exhibition of God's love draws forth emotions in the unregenerate heart that are nothing short of murderous at times. In other cases, God's love is met by callous indifference and criminal ingratitude, as with the nine lepers who never returned to express so much as a word of thanks for their deliverance from a walking death (see Luke 17:12–19).

In the face of divine love being poured forth on Calvary—the holy, sinless God Himself dying for sinful, depraved, undeserving humanity—what is the reaction? Gratitude? Love? Contrition? No! Hate lashes out in jeers and mocking. Violence and cruelty flow forth like a river and mingle with the very blood that was spilt for their redemption!

No. Human kindness will never be enough. It will never fill the twelve baskets with fragments. There will never be any crumbs left over for others unless you first eat from your own personal love feast with the Savior.

Let Him fully satisfy your soul-hunger, and then you will go forth with a full basket on your arm. Twelve baskets there were (see Matthew 14:20). One for each disciple. There will always be the multitudes to be fed, but the few called to minister. This is by My own arrangement. As the Scripture says: "My brethren, let not many of you become teachers, knowing that we shall receive a stricter judgment" (James 3:1).

Many are called. Few are chosen. ☀

Frances J. Roberts is a songwriter, poet, and author of nine books. A graduate of Moody Bible College and a former state director of Child Evangelism Fellowship, Frances also taught at a Spanish mission school and served as a professional accompanist. She lives in Southern California.

Come Away My Beloved
Paper, 256 pages
© 2002 by Frances J. Roberts
Barbour Publishing Inc.
ISBN: 1593100221

∾ THEOLOGY ∾
More Than a Carpenter
Josh McDowell

This hardheaded book is for people who are skeptical about Jesus' deity, resurrection, and claims on their lives.

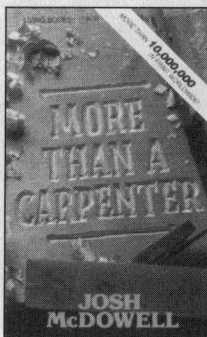

RECENTLY I WAS TALKING with a group of people in Los Angeles. I asked them, "Who, in your opinion, is Jesus Christ?" The response was that he was a great religious leader. I agree with that. Jesus Christ was a great religious leader. But I believe he was much more.

Men and women down through the ages have been divided over the question, "Who is Jesus?"

Why so much conflict over one individual? Why is it that his name, more than the name of any other religious leader, causes irritation? Why is it that you can talk about God and nobody gets upset, but as soon as you mention Jesus, people so often want to stop the conversation? Or they become defensive. I mentioned something about Jesus to a taxicab driver in London, and immediately he said, "I don't like to discuss religion, especially Jesus." How is Jesus different from other religious leaders? Why don't the names of Buddha, Mohammed, Confucius offend people? The reason is that these others didn't claim to be God, but Jesus did. That is what makes him so different from other religious leaders.

It didn't take long for the people who knew Jesus to realize that he was making astounding claims about himself. It became clear that his own claims were identifying him as more than just a prophet or teacher. He was obviously making claims to deity. He was presenting himself as the only avenue to a relationship with God, the only source of forgiveness for sins, and the only way of salvation.

For many people this is too exclusive, too narrow for them to want to believe. Yet the issue is not what do we want to think or believe, but rather, who did Jesus claim to be?

What do the New Testament documents tell us about this? We often hear the phrase, "the deity of

Christ." This means that Jesus Christ is God. A. H. Strong in his Systematic Theology defines God as the "infinite and perfect spirit in whom all things have their source, support, and end."1 This definition of God is adequate for all theists, including Muslims and Jews. Theism teaches that God is personal and that the universe was planned and created by him. God sustains and rules it in the present. Christian theism adds an additional note to the above definition: "and who became incarnate as Jesus of Nazareth."

Jesus Christ is actually a name and a title. The name Jesus is derived from the Greek form of the name Jeshua or Joshua meaning "Jehovah-Savior" or "the Lord saves." The title Christ is derived from the Greek word for Messiah (or the Hebrew Mashiach—Daniel 9:26) and means "anointed one." Two offices, king and priest, are involved in the use of the title "Christ." His title affirms Jesus as the promised priest and king of Old Testament prophecies. This affirmation is one of the crucial areas for having a proper understanding about Jesus and Christianity.

The New Testament clearly presents Christ as God. The names applied to Christ in the New Testament are such that they could properly be applied only to one who was God. For example, Jesus is called God in the phrase, "Looking for the blessed hope and the appearing of the glory of our great God and Savior, Christ Jesus" (Titus

2:13;compare John 1:1; Hebrews 1:8; Romans
9:5; 1 John 5:20-21). The Scriptures attribute
characteristics to him that can be true only of
God. Jesus is presented as being self-existent
(John 1:4; 14:6); omnipresent (Matthew 28:20;
18:20); omniscient (John 4:16; 6:64; Matthew
17:22-27); omnipotent (Revelation 1:8; Luke
4:39-55; 7:14-15; Matthew 8:26-27); and pos-
sessing eternal life (1 John 5:11-12, 20; John 1:4).
Jesus received honor and worship that only God
should receive. In a confrontation with Satan,
Jesus said, "It is written, 'You shall worship the
Lord your God, and serve Him only'" (Matthew
4:10). Yet Jesus received worship as God (Matthew
14:33, 28:9) and sometimes even demanded to be
worshiped as God (John 5:23; compare
Hebrews1:6; Revelation 5:8-14).

Most of the followers of Jesus were devout
Jews who believed in one true God. They were
monotheistic to the core, yet they recognized him as
God Incarnate. Because of his extensive rabbinical
training, Paul would be even less likely to attribute
deity to Jesus, to worship a man from Nazareth and
call him Lord. But this is exactly what Paul did. He
acknowledged the Lamb of God (Jesus) as God
when he said, "Be on guard for yourselves and for
all the flock, among which the Holy Spirit has made
you overseers, to shepherd the church of God which
He purchased with His own blood" (Acts 20:28).
Peter confessed, after Christ asked him who he was:

"Thou art the Christ, the Son of the living God" (Matthew 16:16). Jesus responded to Peter's confession not by correcting his conclusion but by acknowledging its validity and source: "Blessed are you, Simon Barjona, because flesh and blood did not reveal this to you, but My Father who is in heaven" (Matthew 16:17). Martha, a close friend of Jesus, said to him, "I have believed that You are the Christ (Messiah), the Son of God" (John 11:27).

Then there is Nathanael, who didn't think anything good could come out of Nazareth. He acknowledged that Jesus was "the Son of God; you are the King of Israel" (John 1:49). While Stephen was being stoned, "he called upon the Lord and said, 'Lord Jesus, receive my spirit!'" (Acts 7:59). The writer of Hebrews calls Christ God when he writes, "But of the Son He says, 'Thy throne, O God, is forever and ever'" (Hebrews 1:8). John the Baptist announced the coming of Jesus by saying that "the Holy Spirit descended upon Him in bodily form like a dove, and a voice came out of heaven, 'Thou art My beloved Son, in thee I am well-pleased" (Luke 3:22).

Then of course we have the confession of Thomas, better known as "The Doubter." Perhaps he was a graduate student. He said, "I won't believe unless I can put my finger into his nail scars." I identify with Thomas. He said, "Look, not every day does someone raise himself from the dead or claim to be God incarnate. I need evidence." Eight days later, after Thomas chronicled his doubts about Jesus before the other disciples, "Jesus came, the doors having been shut, and stood in their midst, and said, 'Peace be with you.' Then He said to Thomas, 'Reach here your finger, and see My hands; and reach here your hand, and put it into My side; and be not unbelieving, but believing.' Thomas answered and said to Him, 'My Lord and my God!' Jesus said to Him, 'Because you have seen Me, have you believed? Blessed are they who did not see, and yet believed'" (John 20:26-29). Jesus accepted Thomas's acknowledgment of him as God. He rebuked Thomas for his unbelief, but not for his worship.

At this point a critic may interject that all these references are from others about Christ, not from Christ about himself. The accusation in the classroom is usually that those at the time of Christ misunderstood him as we are misunderstanding him today. In other words, Jesus really didn't claim to be God. Well, I think he did, and I believe that the deity of Christ is derived directly from the pages of the New Testament. The references are abundant and their meaning is plain. A businessman who scrutinized the Scriptures to verify whether or not Christ claimed to be God said, "For anyone to read the New Testament and not conclude that Jesus claimed to be divine, he would have to be as blind as a man standing outdoors on a clear day and saying he can't see the sun."

In the Gospel of John we have a confrontation between Jesus and some Jews. It was triggered by Jesus' curing a lame man on the Sabbath and telling him to pick up his pallet and walk. "And for this reason the Jews were persecuting Jesus, because he was doing these things on the Sabbath. But he answered them, 'My Father is working until now, and I Myself am working.' For this cause therefore the Jews were seeking all the more to kill Him, because He not only was breaking the Sabbath, but also was calling God His own Father, making Himself equal with God" (John 5:16-18). You might say, "Look, Josh, I can say, 'My father is working until now, and I myself am working.' So what? It doesn't prove anything." Whenever we study a document, we must take into account the language, the culture, and especially the person or persons addressed. In this case, the culture is Jewish and the persons addressed are Jewish religious leaders. Let's see how the Jews understood Jesus' remarks 2,000 years ago in their own culture. "For this cause therefore the Jews were seeking all the more to kill Him, because He not only was breaking the Sabbath, but also was calling God His own Father, making Himself equal with God" (John 5:18). Why such a drastic reaction?

The reason is that Jesus said "my Father," not "our Father," and then added "is working until now." Jesus' use of these two phrases made himself equal with God, on a par with God's activity. The

Jews did not refer to God as "my Father." Or if they did, they would qualify the statement with "in heaven." However, Jesus did not do this. He made a claim that the Jews could not misinterpret when he called God "my Father." Jesus also implied that while God was working, he, the Son, was working too. Again, the Jews understood the implication that he was God's Son. As a result of this statement, the Jews' hatred grew. Even though they were seeking, mainly, to persecute him, they then began to desire to kill him. Not only did Jesus claim equality with God as his Father, but he also asserted that he was one with the Father. ✶

———————

JOSH MCDOWELL HAS DEVOTED HIS life to telling a doubting world about Christ. A graduate of Wheaton College and Talbot Theological Seminary, he became a traveling representative of Campus Crusade for Christ International. After almost four decades, cutting-edge ministry has become Josh's mantra for reaching skeptics. He has touched the lives of more than 7 million young people in 84 countries. The Josh McDowell Ministry is considered one of the world's largest evangelistic organizations providing humanitarian aid. He has written or co-written 77 books on topics ranging from Christian apologetics to common problems facing youth.

Josh and his wife, Dottie, have partnered in what he consid-

ers his first ministry: family. They have four children and live
in Dallas, TX.

More Than a Carpenter
Paper, 128 pages
© 1977 by Josh McDowell. All rights reserved.
Tyndale House Publishers
ISBN: 0-8423-4552-3

∽ PRAYER ∾

Experiencing the Depths of Jesus Christ
JEANNE GUYON

'If you are starving and can find nothing to satisfy your hunger, then come. Come, and you will be filled.'
—*Jeanne Guyon*

Jeanne Guyon
EXPERIENCING
THE DEPTHS
OF JESUS CHRIST
One of the greatest
Christian writings of all time
Library of Spiritual Classics
Volume 2

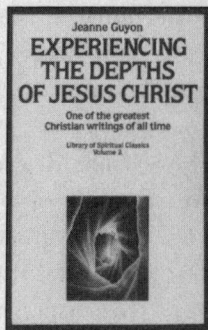

From the Shallows to the Depths

AS YOU PICK UP this book, you may feel that you simply are not one of those people capable of a deep experience with Jesus Christ. Most Christians do not feel that *they* have been called to a deep, inward relationship to their Lord. But we have all been called to the depths of Christ just as surely as we have been called to salvation.

When I speak of this "deep, inward relationship to Jesus Christ," what do I mean? Actually, it is very simple. It is only the turning and yielding of your heart to the Lord. It is the expression of love within your heart for Him.

You will recall that Paul encourages us to "pray without ceasing." (I Thessalonians 5:17) The Lord also invites us to "watch and pray." (Mark 13:33,37) It is apparent from these two verses, as well as many more, that we all live by this kind of experience, this *prayer,* just as we live by love.

Once the Lord spoke and said, "I counsel you to buy from me gold tried in the fire that you may be rich." (Revelation 3:18) Dear reader, there is gold available to *you.* This gold is much more easily obtained than you could ever imagine. It is available to you. The purpose of this book is to launch you into this exploration and into this discovery.

I give you an invitation: If you are thirsty, come to the living waters. Do not waste your precious time digging wells that have no water in them. (John 7:37; Jeremiah 2:13)

If you are starving and can find nothing to satisfy your hunger, then come. Come, and you will be filled.

You who are poor, come.

You who are afflicted, come.

You who are weighted down with your load of

wretchedness and your load of pain, come. You will be comforted!

You who are sick and need a physician, come. Don't hesitate because you have diseases. Come to your Lord and show Him all your diseases, and they will be healed!

Come!

Dear child of God, your Father has His arms of love open wide to you. Throw yourself into His arms. You who have strayed and wandered away as sheep, return to your Shepherd. You who are sinners, come to your Savior.

I especially address those of you who are very simple and you who are uneducated, even you who cannot read and write. You may think you are the one person *most* incapable of this abiding experience of Christ, this prayer of simplicity. You may think yourself the one farthest from a deep experience with the Lord; but, in fact, the Lord has *especially* chosen you! You are the one *most* suited to know Him well.

So let no one feel left out. Jesus Christ has called us all.

Oh, I suppose there *is* one group who is left out!

Do not come if you have no heart. You see, before you come, there is one thing you must do: You must first give your heart to the Lord.

"But I do not know how to give my heart to the Lord."

Well, in this little book you will learn what it means to give your heart to the Lord and how to make that gift to Him.

Let me ask you, then, do you desire to know the Lord in a deep way? God *has* made such an experience, such a walk, possible for you. He has made it possible through the grace He has given to *all* His redeemed children. He has done it by means of His Holy Spirit.

How then will you come to the Lord to know Him in such a deep way? Prayer is the key. But I have in mind a certain kind of prayer. It is a kind of prayer that is very simple and yet holds the key to perfection and goodness—things found only in God Himself. The type of prayer that I have in mind will deliver you from enslavement to every sin. It is a prayer that will release to you every Godly virtue.

You see, the only way to be perfect is to walk in the presence of God. The only way you can live in His presence in uninterrupted fellowship is by means of prayer, but a very special kind of prayer. It is a prayer that leads you into the presence of God and keeps you there at all times; a prayer that can be experienced under any conditions, any place, and any time.

Is there really such a prayer? Does such an experience with Christ truly exist?

Yes, there is such a prayer! A prayer that does not interfere with your outward activities or your daily routine.

There is a kind of prayer that can be practiced by kings, by priests, by soldiers, by laborers, by children, by women, and even by the sick.

May I hasten to say that the kind of prayer I am speaking of is not a prayer that comes from your mind. It is a prayer that begins in the heart. It does not come from your understanding or your thoughts. Prayer offered to the Lord from your mind simply would not be adequate. Why? Because your mind is very limited. The mind can pay attention to only one thing at a time. Prayer that comes out of the heart is not interrupted by thinking! I will go so far as to say that nothing can interrupt this prayer, *the prayer of simplicity*.

Oh yes, there is *one* thing. Selfish desires can cause this prayer to cease. But even here there is encouragement, for once you have enjoyed your Lord and tasted the sweetness of His love, you will find that even your selfish desires no longer hold any power. You will find it impossible to have pleasure in anything except Him.

I realize that some of you may feel that you are very slow, that you have a poor understanding, and that you are very unspiritual. Dear reader, there is nothing in this universe that is easier to obtain than the enjoyment of Jesus Christ! Your Lord is more present to you than you are to yourself! Furthermore, His desire to give Himself to you is *greater* than *your* desire to lay hold of Him.

How, then, do you begin? You need only

one thing. You need only to know how to seek Him. When you have found the way to seek Him, you will discover that this way to God is more natural and easier than taking a breath.

By this "prayer of simplicity," this *experiencing* of Christ deep within, you may live by God Himself with less difficulty and with less interruption than you now live by the air which you take into you. If this is true, then I ask, wouldn't it be a sin not to pray? Yes, it would be a sin. But once you have learned how to seek Jesus Christ and how to lay hold of Him, you will find the way so easy that you will no longer neglect this relationship to your Lord.

Let us go on, therefore, and learn this simple way to pray.

✢ ✢ ✢

We hope you enjoyed reading the first chapter in this classic book on knowing Jesus Christ in a real and deep way.

Below are the remaining chapter titles from *Experiencing the Depths of Jesus Christ* to invite you to plunge into the depths of the Lord.

JEANNE GUYON LIVED DURING THE 1600s and is known as one of the most influential Christian women in church history. This little book appeared in 1685 and is still considered as one of the most helpful and powerful Christian books ever written. Guyon suffered much in her life, and there was a time when this book was publicly burned. On the basis of this book, she was arrested and tried by a religious tribunal. She was denounced as a heretic and imprisoned, eventually, in the infamous Bastille. Jeanne Guyon's writings reveal a Christ-centeredness that has stood the test of time.

EXPERIENCING THE DEPTHS OF JESUS CHRIST
Paper, 160 pages
© 1975 by SeedSowers Publishing House
ISBN: 0-940232-00-6

∽ CHRISTIAN LIVING ∾
Desiring God
JOHN PIPER

In this paradigm-
smashing classic, newly
revised and expanded,
John Piper reveals the
debate between duty and
delight doesn't truly exist:
Delight is our duty.

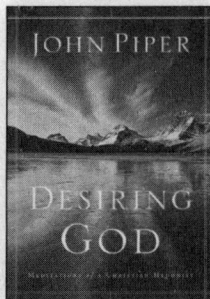

WHEN I WAS IN college, I had a vague, pervasive
notion that if I did something good because it
would make me happy, I would ruin its goodness.

I figured that the goodness of my moral action
was lessened to the degree that I was motivated by a
desire for my own pleasure. At the time, buying ice
cream in the student center just for pleasure didn't

bother me, because the moral consequences of that action seemed so insignificant. But to be motivated by a desire for happiness or pleasure when I volunteered for Christian service or went to church—that seemed selfish, utilitarian, mercenary.

This was a problem for me because I couldn't formulate an alternative motive that worked. I found in myself an overwhelming longing to be happy, a tremendously powerful impulse to seek pleasure, yet at every point of moral decision I said to myself that this impulse should have no influence.

One of the most frustrating areas was that of worship and praise. My vague notion that the higher the activity, the less there must be of self-interest in it caused me to think of worship almost solely in terms of duty. And that cuts the heart out of it.

Then I was converted to Christian Hedonism. In a matter of weeks I came to see that it is unbiblical and arrogant to try to worship God for any other reason than the pleasure to be had in Him. (Don't miss those last two words: *in Him*. Not His gifts, but Him. Not ourselves, but Him.) Let me describe the series of insights that made me a Christian Hedonist. Along the way, I hope it will become clear what I mean by this strange phrase.

1. During my first quarter in seminary, I was introduced to the argument for Christian Hedonism and one of its great exponents, Blaise Pascal. He wrote:

> All men seek happiness. This is without excep-
> tion. Whatever different means they employ,
> they all tend to this end. The cause of some
> going to war, and of others avoiding it, is the
> same desire in both, attended with different
> views. The will never takes the least step but to
> this object. This is the motive of every action of
> every man, even of those who hang themselves.[1]

This statement so fit with my own deep longings, and all that I had ever seen in others, that I
accepted it and have never found any reason to
doubt it. What struck me especially was that Pascal
was not making any moral judgment about this fact.
As far as he was concerned, seeking one's own happiness is not a sin; it is a simple given in human
nature. It is a law of the human heart, as gravity is a
law of nature.

This thought made great sense to me and
opened the way for the second discovery.

2. I had grown to love the works of C. S. Lewis
in college. But not until later did I buy the sermon
called "The Weight of Glory." The first page of that
sermon is one of the most influential pages of literature I have ever read. It goes like this:

> If you asked twenty good men today what they

---

1. Blaise Pascal, *Pascal's Pensees*, trans. W. F. Trotter (New York: E. P.
   Dutton, 1958), 113, thought #425.

thought the highest of the virtues, nineteen of
them would reply, Unselfishness. But if you
asked almost any of the great Christians of old
he would have replied, Love. You see what has
happened? A negative term has been substi-
tuted for a positive, and this is of more than
philological importance. The negative ideal
of Unselfishness carries with it the suggestion
not primarily of securing good things for
others, but of going without them ourselves,
as if our abstinence and not their happiness
was the important point. I do not think this is
the Christian virtue of Love. The New
Testament has lots to say about self-denial,
but not about self-denial as an end in itself.
We are told to deny ourselves and to take up
our crosses in order that we may follow
Christ; and nearly every description of what
we shall ultimately find if we do so contains an
appeal to desire.

If there lurks in most modern minds the
notion that to desire our own good and
earnestly to hope for the enjoyment of it is a
bad thing, I submit that this notion has crept in
from Kant and the Stoics and is no part of the
Christian faith. Indeed, if we consider the
unblushing promises of reward and the stag-
gering nature of the rewards promised in the
Gospels, it would seem that Our Lord finds

our desires not too strong, but too weak. We are half-hearted creatures, fooling about with drink and sex and ambition when infinite joy is offered us, like an ignorant child who wants to go on making mud pies in a slum because he cannot imagine what is meant by the offer of a holiday at the sea. We are far too easily pleased.[2]

There it was in black and white, and to my mind it was totally compelling: It is not a bad thing to desire our own good. In fact, the great problem of human beings is that they are far too easily pleased. They don't seek pleasure with nearly the resolve and passion that they should. And so they settle for mud pies of appetite instead of infinite delight.

I had never in my whole life heard any Christian, let alone a Christian of Lewis's stature, say that all of us not only seek (as Pascal said), but also *ought to seek,* our own happiness. Our mistake lies not in the intensity of our desire for happiness, but in the weakness of it.

3. The third insight was there in Lewis's sermon, but Pascal made it more explicit. He goes on to say:

There once was in man a true happiness of which now remain to him only the mark and

---

2. C. S. Lewis, *The Weight of Glory and Other Addresses* (Grand Rapids, Mich.: Eerdmans, 1965), 1–2.

empty trace, which he in vain tries to fill from all his surroundings, seeking from things absent the help he does not obtain in things present. But these are all inadequate, because the infinite abyss can only be filled by an infinite and immutable object, that is to say, only by God Himself.[3]

As I look back on it now, it seems so patently obvious that I don't know how I could have missed it. All those years I had been trying to suppress my tremendous longing for happiness so I could honestly praise God out of some "higher," less selfish motive. But now it started to dawn on me that this persistent and undeniable yearning for happiness was not to be suppressed, but to be glutted—on God! The growing conviction that praise should be motivated solely by the happiness we find in God seemed less and less strange.

4. The next insight came again from C. S. Lewis, but this time from his *Reflections on the Psalms.* Chapter 9 of this book bears the modest title "A Word about Praise." In my experience it has been *the* word about praise—the best word on the nature of praise I have ever read.

Lewis says that as he was beginning to believe in God, a great stumbling block was the presence of

---

3. Pascal, Pensees, 113.

demands scattered through the Psalms that he should praise God. He did not see the point in all this; besides, it seemed to picture God as craving "for our worship like a vain woman who wants compliments." He goes on to show why he was wrong:

> But the most obvious fact about praise— whether of God or anything—strangely escaped me. I thought of it in terms of compliment, approval, or the giving of honor. I had never noticed that all enjoyment spontaneously overflows into praise....
>
> I think we delight to praise what we enjoy because the praise not merely expresses but completes the enjoyment; it is its appointed consummation.[4]

This was the capstone of my emerging Hedonism. Praising God, the highest calling of humanity and our eternal vocation, did not involve the renunciation, but rather the consummation of the joy I so desired. My old effort to achieve worship with no self-interest in it proved to be a contradiction in terms. God is not worshiped where He is not treasured and enjoyed. Praise is not an alternative to joy, but the expression of joy. Not to enjoy God is to dishonor Him. To say to Him that something else satisfies you

---

4. C. S. Lewis, *Reflections on the Psalms* (New York: Harcourt, Brace & World, 1958), 94–5.

more is the opposite of worship. It is sacrilege.

I saw this not only in C. S. Lewis, but also in the eighteenth-century pastor Jonathan Edwards. No one had ever taught me that God is glorified by our joy in Him. That joy in God is the very thing that makes praise an honor to God, and not hypocrisy. But Edwards said so clearly and powerfully:

> God glorifies Himself toward the creatures...by...communicating Himself to their hearts, and in their rejoicing and delighting in, and enjoying, the manifestations which He makes of Himself.... *God is glorified not only by His glory's being seen, but by its being rejoiced in.* When those that see it delight in it, God is more glorified than if they only see it....[5]

This was a stunning discovery for me. I *must* pursue joy in God if I am to glorify Him as the surpassingly valuable Reality in the universe. Joy is not a mere option alongside worship. It is an essential component of worship.[6]

We have a name for those who try to praise

---

5. Jonathan Edwards, "Miscellanies," in *The Works of Jonathan Edwards*, vol. 13, ed. Thomas Schafer (New Haven: Yale University Press, 1994), 495, miscellany #448, emphasis added. See also #87 (pp. 251–2); #332 (p. 410); #679 (not in the New Haven volume).

6. I will deal in chapter 4 with the place of sadness in the Christian life and how it can be a part of worship, which is never perfect in this age. True evangelical brokenness for sin is a sadness experienced only by those who taste the pleasures of God's goodness and feel the regret that they do not savor it as fully as they ought.

when they have no pleasure in the object. We call
them hypocrites. This fact—that praise means consummate pleasure and that the highest end of man
is to drink deeply of this pleasure—was perhaps the
most liberating discovery I ever made.

5. Then I turned to the Psalms for myself and
found the language of Hedonism everywhere. The
quest for pleasure was not even optional, but com-
manded: "Delight yourself in the Lord, and he will
give you the desires of your heart" (Psalm 37:4).

The psalmists sought to do just this: "As a
deer pants for flowing streams, so pants my soul for
you, O God. My soul thirsts for God, for the living
God" (Psalm 42:1–2). "My soul thirsts for you; my
flesh faints for you, as in a dry and weary land where
there is no water" (Psalm 63:1). The motif of thirst-
ing has its satisfying counterpart when the psalmist
says that men "drink their fill of the abundance of
Your house; and You give them to drink of the river
of Your delights" (Psalm 36:8, NASB).

I found that the goodness of God, the very
foundation of worship, is not a thing you pay your
respects to out of some kind of disinterested reverence. No, it is something to be enjoyed: "Oh, taste
and see that the Lord is good!" (Psalm 34:8). "How
sweet are your words to my taste, sweeter than honey
to my mouth!" (Psalm 119:103).

As C. S. Lewis says, God in the Psalms is the
"all-satisfying Object." His people adore Him

unashamedly for the "exceeding joy" they find in Him (Psalm 43:4). He is the source of complete and unending pleasure: "In your presence there is fullness of joy; at your right hand are pleasures forevermore" (Psalm 16:11).

That is the short story of how I became a Christian Hedonist. I have now been brooding over these things for some thirty-five years, and there has emerged a philosophy that touches virtually every area of my life. I believe that it is biblical, that it fulfills the deepest longings of my heart, and that it honors the God and Father of our Lord Jesus Christ. I have written this book to commend these things to all who will listen. ✳

JOHN PIPER RECEIVED HIS DOCTORATE in theology from the University of Munich and taught biblical studies for six years at Bethel College. The author of numerous books, he has been pastor of Bethlehem Baptist Church in Minneapolis since 1980. He and his wife, Noël, have four sons and one daughter.

DESIRING GOD
Paper, 358 pages
Adapted from Desiring God © 1986, 1996, 2003 by
Desiring God Foundation. Used by permission of
Multnomah Publishers, Inc. All rights reserved.
ISBN: 1-59052-119-6

∽ CHRISTIAN LIVING ∽
Love Must Be Tough
JAMES DOBSON

Love Must Be Tough
offers hope and a strategic, respect-based plan for restoring your marriage with Dr. Dobson's time-tested advice.

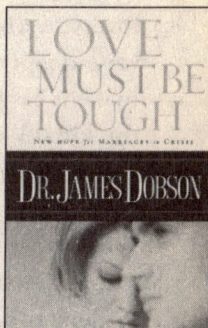

Introduction

SIT DOWN, CAROL. I have to talk to you about something very serious. I know what I'm going to say will come as a shock to you, but I can't withhold the truth any longer. You deserve to know that I've been involved in an affair with a woman at the office for nearly eighteen months. Her name is Brenda and she is very attractive. It started as an innocent flirtation, but quickly progressed into something more—much more. Now we are unable to pretend any longer. That's why I've made an appointment with an attorney, and I plan to divorce you as quickly as possible. I'm sorry! Honestly, I am. What more can I say? I never intended to hurt you. But I just don't love you any longer—and I do love Brenda—very deeply. So, Carol, I'm asking you to make it easy for both of us, and of course, for the kids. We'll all be better off as soon as this mess is settled.

With those words, the world falls off its axis for an unsuspecting woman and the children who can't understand why she cries. Suddenly, everything stable in their lives has been shattered. Rejection and insult are blended with pain and remorse. Self-esteem collapses like a grand old building scheduled for demolition. Security and confidence give way to fear and anxiety. The future loses its significance. But most disturbing of all, the woman who felt loved and respected a few hours before now feels utterly disdained and unlovable.

How common this set of circumstances has become in the Western world, not only for the Carols and Jeannies and Patricias around us, but also for the Robs and Toms and Carls. Whether for reasons of infidelity or because of one of the other great marriage killers, many husbands and wives find themselves being dragged relentlessly toward an unwanted divorce. For some, the realization does not come as a startling "announcement" like the one that shattered Carol. Rather, they watch helplessly as their marriages wither over a period of years, being consumed by an insidious cancer that gnaws at the soul of the relationship. They turn this way and that, searching desperately for answers—solutions—remedies. Unfortunately—and this is the critical point—the advice they are given by friends and even counselors is often disastrous in its effect.

The book you are about to read provides an alternative for those in the midst of family crises. My purpose in writing it has been to offer some practical tools—some understandings—which should be useful in drawing an apathetic husband or wife back in the direction of commitment. It may be surprising to learn that human conflict, if properly managed, can be the vehicle for transforming an unstable relationship into a vibrant, healthy marriage. On the other hand, the wrong response in moments of crisis can quickly smother the dying embers of love.

I should acknowledge at the outset that some of the principles I will offer may be controversial within Christian circles. It is my belief that the advice traditionally offered to victims of infidelity and other violations of trust has often been unbiblical and destructive. But obviously, not everyone will agree. To those who draw differing conclusions, I can only ask for charity as we seek to resolve the most difficult family problems with our limited knowledge and insight.

But that's enough for now. Let me offer one precaution before we proceed. If you are a husband or wife who is steadily losing the one you love—if you sense a growing disrespect and disdain from the most important person in your world—this book is intended for your eyes only. Do not ask your partner to read it with you. At least, you should review it first and then decide for yourself whether or not to reveal its message....

Thank you for permitting me to share some new concepts with you. I hope you will find them helpful, even if you do not have a family in crisis.

With Love to the Victims

More than one hundred thousand letters and hundreds of telephone calls pour through our Focus on the Family offices each month, representing the full range of human circumstance and need.... Included in that mail recently was a poignant letter from a man I'll call Roger.* His story moved me deeply.

A few months ago, my wife, Norma, left

---
*All the letters quoted in this book have been modified to protect the names and identities of the writers.

to go to the grocery store in a nearby shopping center. She told our four children that she would be back in half an hour and warned them to behave themselves. That occurred on Saturday morning. Six hours later she had not returned, and I began a frantic search for her. I could imagine her being kidnapped or raped or even something worse. By Sunday morning I called the Detroit police, but they said they could not help until she had been gone forty-eight hours. The children and I were worried sick!

We requested prayer from our church and Christian friends, especially for Norma's safety. She had left no notes or messages with friends, and she didn't call. We did find her car behind the shopping center, locked and empty. The police theorized that she had run away, but I didn't agree. That just wasn't like the woman I had lived with for fourteen years...the mother of my four children. We had been getting along quite well, actually, and had been planning to take a brief vacation over the Labor Day weekend.

On Tuesday, I obtained the services of a well-known police detective and asked him to help us locate my wife—or at least discover what had happened to her. Well, he began interviewing her friends and associates and the details unfolded. To my utter shock, it became clear that Norma had left of her own free will with a married man from her place of employment. I just couldn't believe it.

Then about two weeks later, I got a "Dear John" letter, saying she didn't love me anymore—that our marriage was finished. Just like that, it was over. She said she would be returning in a few months to fight for the children, and that they would be living with her in Kansas.

Dr. Dobson, I tell you truthfully that I have always been a faithful father and husband. Even since my wife left, I have taken good care of the kids. I did the best I could to pull our lives together and keep going...to try to make a decent home for these four bewildered youngsters. Nevertheless, the court ruled in my wife's favor last month, and now I am alone.

I built our house a few years ago with my own hands, and now it is empty! All I have to show for the family I lost is a stack of Norma's bills and the memories that were born in these walls. My kids will be raised in an un-Christian home, five hundred miles away, and I hardly have enough money to even visit them!

My life is a shambles now. I have nothing but free time to think about the woman I love...and the hurt and rejection I feel. It is an awful experience. Norma has destroyed me. I will never recover. I am lonely and depressed. I wake up in the night thinking about what might have been...and what is. Only God can help me now!

I wish this letter from Roger represented a rare tragedy that occurred only in the most unusual of circumstances. Unfortunately, variations on this theme are increasingly common today. Sexual intrigue has become a familiar pattern in today's marriages, not only outside the framework of the Christian church but within it as well. And, of course, the most vulnerable victims of family instability are the children who are too young to understand what has happened to their parents.

That tragic impact on the next generation was graphically illustrated to me in a recent conversation with a sixth-grade teacher in an upper middle-class California city. She was shocked to see the results of a creative writing task assigned to her students. They were asked to complete a sentence that began with the words "I wish." The teacher expected the boys and girls to express wishes for bicycles, dogs, television sets and trips to Hawaii. Instead, twenty of the thirty children made reference in their responses to their own disintegrating families. A few of their actual sentences were as follows:

I wish my parents wouldn't fight and I

wish my father would come back.

I wish my mother didn't have a boyfriend.

I wish I could get straight A's so my father would love me.

I wish I had one mom and one dad so the kids wouldn't make fun of me. I have three moms and three dads and they botch up my life.

I wish I had an m-1 rifle so I could shoot those who make fun of me.

I know it's hardly front page news to announce that the family is in trouble today, but it will always distress me to see little children like these struggling with such chaos at a time when simply growing up is a major undertaking. Millions of their peers are caught in the same snare.

Consider the plight of Roger's children in the letter I shared. First, they lost their mother, then watched their father immersed in grief and agony, and finally found themselves jerked from familiar surroundings and transplanted into another state with a new guy who wanted to be called "Dad." They will never be the same! And why was this upheaval necessary? Because their mother cared more about her own happiness and welfare than she did about theirs. As a young woman, she had stood at an altar before God and man, solemnly promising to love and to cherish Roger—for better or worse, for richer or poorer, in sickness and health, forsaking all others, till separated by the hand of death. Unfortunately, Norma changed her mind....

The book you hold is dedicated, therefore, to that vulnerable member of the family who can be thought of as a victim in extreme cases. This is the only text of which I am aware whose primary purpose is to help a distressed person strengthen or preserve his or her marriage, even in the absence of a willing spouse.... What about the woman who loves her husband and is loved by him in return, but worries about the total absence of romantic excitement between them? Is there any way she can heat up their relationship without nagging her husband incessantly?

Virtually every counseling program now in existence for such families is designed to bring together two people who can agree, at least, to discuss their problems. Or if therapy is offered for a single partner, it is directed at strengthening that individual to cope with the crisis and go it alone, if necessary. But our purpose here is unique: We want to help one spouse maximize the chances of preserving the marriage and to survive till the long night is over. It's an ambitious undertaking....

But the concepts I will share have even broader applicability than the interaction between husbands and wives. As we will see, they are relevant to all human relationships, including employers and employees, parents and children, pastors and parishioners, business and labor, guards and prisoners, Americans and Russians, and all the other categories of people who share an interface from time to time. In other words, I will be describing in subsequent chapters what I consider to be some universal concepts that cut across cultures, sexes, races, and economic circumstances. And unless I have missed the mark, they will hit somewhere near your neck of the woods in one context or another. ☀

DR. JAMES DOBSON IS THE founder and president of Focus on the Family, a nonprofit organization whose internationally syndicated radio programs are heard by 200 million listeners daily. A licensed psychologist and marriage, family, and child counselor, Dr. Dobson is the author of numerous top-selling books dedicated to the preservation of the family. He and his wife, Shirley, are the parents of two grown children and live in Colorado Springs, CO.

LOVE MUST BE TOUGH
Paper, 238 pages
Adapted from Love Must be Tough © 1983, 1996 by James Dobson, Inc. Used by permission of Multnomah Publishers Inc. All rights reserved.
ISBN: 1-59052-355-5

∽ S P I R I T U A L   G R O W T H ∽

Love Not the World
WATCHMAN NEE

Nee shows that all
worldly systems move
away from God. How
then can Christians work
within the world and
not be "of the world"?

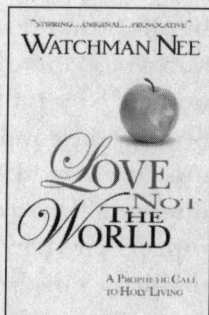

EVERY ONE OF US having been in bondage to sin, we readily believe that sinful things are Satanic; but do we believe equally that the things of the world are Satanic? Many of us, I think, are still of two minds about this. Yet how clearly Scripture affirms that "the whole world lieth in the evil one" (1 John 5:19). Satan well knows that, generally speaking, to try to ensnare real Christians through things that

are positively sinful is vain and futile. They will usually sense the danger and elude him. So he has
contrived instead an enticing network, the mesh of
which is so skillfully woven as to entrap the most
innocent of men. We flee sinful lusts, and with good
reason, but when it comes to such seemingly
innocuous things as science and art and education,
how readily do we lose our sense of values and fall a
prey to his enticements!

Yet our Lord's sentence of judgment clearly
implies that everything that constitutes "the
world" is out of line with God's purpose. His
words, "Now is the judgment of this world," clearly imply the condemnation of all that goes to make
up "the world," and would never have been
uttered if there were not something radically amiss
with it. Further, when Jesus goes on: "Now shall
the prince of this world be cast out," he is stressing not merely the intimate relation between
Satan and the world order but the fact that its
condemnation is linked with his. Do we acknowledge that Satan is today the prince of education
and science and culture and the arts, and that
they, with him, are doomed? Do we acknowledge
that he is the effective master of all those things
that together make up the world system?

When mention is made of a dance hall or a
night club, our reaction as Christians is one of
instinctive disapproval. To us that is "the world" *par
excellence.* When, however, to go to the other extreme,

medical science or social service are discussed, there
may be no such reaction at all. These things command our tacit approval, and maybe our
enthusiastic support. And between these extremes
there lies a host of other things varying widely in
their influence for good or bad, between which
none of us would probably agree on where to draw
an exact line. Yet let us face the fact that judgment
has been pronounced by God, not upon certain
selected things that belong to this world, but impar-
tially upon them all.

Test yourself. If you venture into one of these
approved fields, and then someone exclaims to you,
"You have touched the world there," will you be
moved? Probably not at all. It takes someone whom
you really respect to say to you very straightly and
earnestly, "Brother, you have become involved with
Satan there!" before you will so much as hesitate. Is
that not so? How would you feel if anyone said to
you, "You have touched education there," or "You
have touched medical science," or "You have
touched commerce"? Would you react with the
same degree of caution as you would if he had said,
"You have touched the Devil there"? If we truly
believe that whenever we touch any of these things
that constitute the world we touch the prince of this
world, then the awful seriousness of being in any
wise involved in worldly things could not fail to
strike home to us. "The whole world lieth in the evil
one"—not a part of it, but *the whole.* Do not let us

think for a moment that Satan opposes God only by means of sin and carnality in men's hearts; he opposes God by means of every worldly thing. Oh, I agree with you that the things of the world are all in one sense material, lifeless, intrinsically without power to harm us; yet even that itself should suggest that they are resistant to the purpose of God, as indeed is everything in which there is no touch of divine life.

The recurring phrase "after its kind" in Genesis I represents a law of reproduction that governs the whole realm of biological nature. It does not, however, govern the realm of the Spirit. For generation after generation, human parents can beget children after their kind; but one thing is certain: Christians cannot beget Christians! Not even where both parents are Christians will the children born to them automatically be Christians, no, not even in the first generation. It will take a fresh act of God every time.

And this principle applies no less truly in the affairs of mankind more widely. All that belongs to human nature continues spontaneously; all that belongs to God continues only for as long as God's working continues. And the world is all-inclusively that which can continue apart from divine activity, that is, which can go on by itself without the need of specific acts of God to maintain it in freshness. The world, and all that belongs to the world, does this naturally—it is its nature—and in doing so *it moves in a direction contrary to the will of God.* This statement we shall now seek to illustrate both from the Scripture and from Christian experience.

Let us take first the field of political science. The Old Testament history of Israel affords us the example of a highly privileged nation and its government. The people of Israel, we are told, wanted to be on equal terms with the nations around them; so they set their heart on a king. We will leave aside for the moment their election of Saul, and move on to the point where eventually, in his own time, God gave them the king of his choice who would establish the kingdom under his own direction.

Now even when this was clearly God's doing, the natural trend of this kingdom proved to be, "like the nations," away from him. For a kingdom is a worldly thing, and in keeping with all worldly things it tends to come into collision with the divine purpose. Wherever in the world a nation's government is left to itself, it follows its natural course which is further and further away from God. And what is true in secular national politics worked itself out equally surely even in divinely chosen Israel. Whenever God discontinued his specific acts on their behalf, the kingdom of Israel drifted into idolatrous political alignments. There were recoveries, it is true, but every one was marked by a definite divine intervention, and without such intervention the trend was always downhill.

It will scarcely surprise us that the same thing

proves to be true in the field of commerce. I can think of no sphere where the temptation to dishonest and corrupt dealing is so great as here. We all know something of this. We all know how hard it is to remain straight and to conduct affairs honestly in the competitive world of trade. Many would say that it is impossible, and certainly to do so calls for a life that is cast upon God in an unusual way.

We recall that our Lord Jesus tells us of two contrasting men, one who gained the whole world and forfeited his life, and another, a merchant, who went and sold all that he had to buy one priceless pearl. To the latter of these Jesus likened the kingdom of heaven (Matt. 16:26; 13:45-46). The Spirit of God has not infrequently moved men in business to action of a like character. There have been not a few well-known business firms whose profits have been turned over to divine ends in the spread of the gospel and in other ways.

I think of one such enterprise that, at the outset of its history, was the creation of a God-fearing businessman. Now, godly fear is a quality that can exist only as it is sustained from heaven, but business acumen and the efficient organization which it creates can be self-perpetuating. In the first generation of this firm's history we find divine life being mediated through its founder sufficient to hold what was even then a worldly concern securely under the authority of God. But by the second generation that restraint was gone and, as one would expect, the business gravitated automatically into the world system. Godly fear had drained away, but the firm itself is still flourishing.

Suppose we take now so apparently innocent a matter as agriculture. Here Genesis, written in a primitive world of flocks and husbandry, has something to tell us. After Adam's fall, God was compelled to say to him, "Cursed is the ground for thy sake; in toil shalt thou eat of it all the days of thy life; thorns also and thistles shall it bring forth to thee; and thou shalt eat the herb of the field; in the sweat of thy face shalt thou eat bread, till thou return unto the ground." No one would suggest that in Eden, where the tree of life flourished, farming or gardening was wrong. It was God appointed. But as soon as it was let go from under the hand of God it deteriorated. Man was condemned to an endless round of drudgery and disappointment, and an element of perversity marked the fruit of his toil. The deliverance of Noah was God's great recovery movement, in which the earth was given a fresh start. But how swift, how tragic was man's reversion to type! "Noah began to be a husbandman, and planted a vineyard: and he drank of the wine, and was drunken; and he was uncovered within his tent." Of course, agriculture is not in itself sinful, but here already its direction is away from God. Just let it follow its natural tendency and it will contrive to take a course diametrically opposed to him. Do we know something of this today in such physical disasters as the drying out of continents?

How different is the Church, God's husbandry! Through the grace of God and the indwelling Spirit she possesses an inherent life-power capable, if she responds to it, of keeping her constantly moving Godward, or of recalling her Godward if she strays.

When we turn to education, both the Bible and experience have something to say to us. Speaking allegorically we might say that in rejecting Saul and choosing David, God was passing over a man distinguished by his head (for he was that much taller than his peers) in favor of the man after his heart! But, more seriously, the men such as Joseph and Moses and Daniel, of whose wisdom God made public use, each received in a direct way from God himself the understanding they needed. They took little account of their secular education. And the apostle Paul clearly placed scholarship among the "all things" that he counted to be loss for the excellency of the knowledge of Christ Jesus his Lord (Phil. 3:8). He draws a clear distinction between the wisdom of the world and the wisdom that comes from God (1 Cor. 1:21, 30).

But it is experience that demonstrates the essential worldliness of scholarship as such. Most of the historic university colleges of the West were founded by Christian men with a desire to provide their fellows with a good education under

Christian influence. During their founders' life-times the tone of those foundations was high, because these men put real spiritual content into them. When, however, the men themselves passed away, the spiritual control passed away too, and education followed its inevitable course toward the world of materialism and away from God. In some cases it may have taken a long time, for religious tradition dies hard; but the tendency has always been obvious, and in most cases the destination has by now been reached. When material things are under spiritual control they fulfill their proper subordinate role. Released from that restraint they manifest very quickly the power that lies behind them. The law of their nature asserts itself, and their worldly character is proved by the course they take. ☀

WATCHMAN NEE CAME TO CHRIST at age 19. He dedicated his life to the Lord's work and began his preaching ministry while a university student. From 1923 to 1950, he founded 200 churches in China. These self-supporting congregations became very strong spiritually and grew rapidly. Nee concentrated on deepening spiritual life through intensive training in the Word of God. The Communists, unable to gain his cooperation, imprisoned him from 1950 to 1972.

Nee's rich spoken ministry influenced many lives, and his

stirring messages continue to impact lives through his many
books.

LOVE NOT THE WORLD
Paper, 118 pages
© 1968 Angus I. Kinnear
CLC Publications
ISBN: 0-87508-787-6

⮘ CHRISTIAN LIVING ⮚
The Calvary Road
ROY HESSION

*Do you long for revival
and power in your life?
Learn how through
brokenness, repentance,
and confession, Jesus
can fill you with
His Spirit.*

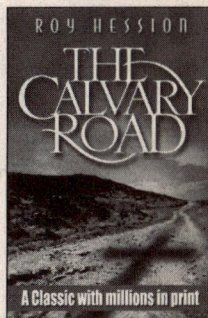

ROY HESSION
THE
CALVARY
ROAD
A Classic with millions in print

WE WANT TO BE very simple in this matter of revival.
Revival is just the life of the Lord Jesus poured into
human hearts. Jesus is always victorious. In heaven
they are praising Him all the time for His victory.
Whatever may be our experience of failure and
barrenness, He is never defeated. His power is
boundless. And we, on our part, have only to get

into a right relationship with Him and we shall see His power being demonstrated in our hearts and lives and service, and His victorious life will fill us and overflow through us to others. And that is revival in its essence.

If, however, we are to come into this right relationship with Him, the first thing we must learn is that our wills must be broken to His will. To be broken is the beginning of revival. It is painful, it is humiliating, but it is the only way. It is being "Not *I*, but *C*hrist," and a "*C*" is a bent "*I*." The Lord Jesus cannot live in us fully and reveal Himself through us until the proud self within us is broken. This simply means that the hard unyielding self, which justifies itself, wants its own way, stands up for its rights, and seeks its own glory, at last bows its head to God's will, admits its wrong, gives up its own way to Jesus, surrenders its rights and discards its own glory—that the Lord Jesus might have all and be all. In other words, it is dying to self and self-attitudes.

And as we look honestly at our Christian lives, we can see how much of this self there is in each of us. It is so often self who tries to live the Christian life (the mere fact that we use the word "try" indicates that it is self who has the responsibility). It is self, too, who is often doing Christian work. It is always self who gets irritable and envious and resentful and critical and worried. It is self who is hard and unyielding in its attitudes to others. It is self who is shy and self-conscious and reserved. No wonder we need breaking. As long as self is in control, God can do little with us, for the fruit of the Spirit (enumerated in Galatians 5) with which God longs to fill us is the complete antithesis of the hard, unbroken spirit within us and presupposes that self has been crucified.

Being broken is both God's work and ours. He brings His pressure to bear, but we have to make the choice. If we are really open to conviction as we seek fellowship with God (and willingness for the light is the prime condition of fellowship with God), God will show us the expressions of this proud, hard self that cause Him pain. Then it is we can stiffen our necks and refuse to repent, or we can bow the head and say, "Yes, Lord." Brokenness in daily experience is simply the response of humility to the conviction of God. And inasmuch as this conviction is continuous, we shall need to be broken continually. And this can be very costly, when we see all the yielding of rights and selfish interests that this will involve, and the confessions and restitutions that may be sometimes necessary.

For this reason, we are not likely to be broken except at the cross of Jesus. The willingness of Jesus to be broken for us is the all-compelling motive in our being broken too. We see Him, who is in the form of God, counting not equality with God a prize to be grasped at and hung on to, but letting it go for us and taking upon Him the form of a Servant—God's Servant, man's Servant. We see Him willing to have no rights of His own, willing to let men revile Him and not revile again, willing to let men tread on Him and not retaliate or defend Himself. Above all, we see Him broken as He meekly goes to Calvary to become men's scapegoat by bearing their sins in His own body on the Tree. In a pathetic passage in a prophetic psalm, He says, "I am a worm, and no man." Those who have been in tropical lands tell us that there is a big difference between a snake and a worm, when you attempt to strike at them. The snake rears itself up and hisses and tries to strike back—a true picture of self. But a worm offers no resistance, it allows you to do what you like with it, kick it or squash it under your heel—a picture of true brokenness. And Jesus was willing to become just that for us—a worm and no man. And He did so, because that is what He saw us to be, worms having forfeited all rights by our sin, except to deserve hell. And He now calls us to take our rightful place as worms for Him and with Him. The whole Sermon on the Mount with its teaching of non-retaliation, love for enemies and selfless giving, assumes that to be our position. But only the vision of the Love that was willing to be broken for us can constrain us to be willing for that.

> Lord, bend that proud and stiffnecked I,
> Help me to bow the head and die;
> Beholding Him on Calvary,
> Who bowed His head for me.

But dying to self is not a thing we do once for all. There may be an initial dying when God first shows these things, but ever after it will be a constant dying, for only so can the Lord Jesus be revealed constantly through us. All day long the choice will be before us in a thousand ways.

It will mean no plans, no time, no money, no pleasure of our own. It will mean a constant yielding to those around us, for our yieldedness to God is measured by our yieldedness to man. Every humiliation, everyone who tries and vexes us, is God's way of breaking us, so that there is a yet deeper channel in us for the Life of Christ.

You see, the only life that pleases God and that can be victorious is His life—never our life, no matter how hard we try. But inasmuch as our self-centered life is the exact opposite of His, we can never be filled with His life unless we are prepared for God to bring our life constantly to death. And in that we must co-operate by our moral choice.

Brokenness, however, is but the beginning of revival. Revival itself is being absolutely filled to overflowing with the Holy Spirit, and that is victorious living. If we were asked this moment if we were filled with the Holy Spirit, how many of us would dare to answer "yes"? Revival is when we can say "yes" at any moment of the day. It is not egotistic to say so, for filling to overflowing is utterly and completely God's work—it is all of grace. All we have to do is to present our empty, broken self and let Him fill and keep filled. Andrew Murray says, "Just as water ever seeks and fills the lowest place, so the moment God finds you abased and empty, His glory and power flow in." The picture that has made things simple and clear to so many of us is that of the human heart as a cup, which we hold out to Jesus, longing that He might fill it with the Water of Life. Jesus is pictured as bearing the golden water pot with the Water of Life. As He passes by He looks into our cup, and if it is clean, He fills it to overflowing with the Water of Life. And as Jesus is always passing by, the cup can be always running over. That is something of what David meant, when he said, "My cup runneth over." This is revival—the constant peace of God ruling in our hearts because we are full to overflowing ourselves, and sharing it with others. People imagine that dying to self makes one miserable. But it is just the opposite. It is the refusal to die to self that makes one miserable. The more we know of death with Him, the more we shall know of His life in us, and so the more of real peace and joy. His life, too, will overflow through us to lost souls in a real concern for their salvation, and to our fellow Christians in a deep desire for their blessing. ✻

ROY HESSION, A SUCCESSFUL EVANGELIST in England, knew he had lost the power of the Spirit in his life—a terrible feeling as he led his evangelistic campaigns. In 1947, he met leaders of the East African church, which was then experiencing a sweeping revival, and recognized his deep personal need. It was like starting the Christian life over as he came humbly to the Cross. The principles which the Lord taught him were first published in 1950 as *The Calvary Road* and are now available in more than 70 languages. Hession's other titles include *We Would See Jesus* and *Be Filled Now*.

THE CALVARY ROAD
Paper, 112 pages
© 1950 Christian Literature Crusade, London
CLC Publications
ISBN: 0-87508-788-4

CHRISTIAN LIVING

The New Evidence That Demands a Verdict

JOSH McDOWELL

*If the New Testament
records about Jesus are
historically accurate,
only three logical
choices remain: He is
a liar, a lunatic,
or Lord of all.*

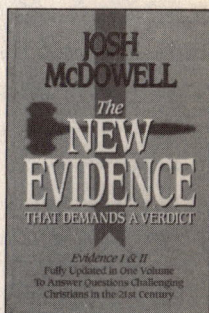

JOSH McDOWELL
The NEW EVIDENCE
THAT DEMANDS A VERDICT
Evidence I & II
Fully Updated in One Volume
To Answer Questions Challenging
Christians in the 21st Century

Significance of Deity: The Trilemma—Lord, Liar, or Lunatic?

1 A. Who Is Jesus of Nazareth?

THROUGHOUT HISTORY, PEOPLE HAVE given a variety of answers to the question, "Who is Jesus of Nazareth?" Whatever their answer, no one can escape the fact that Jesus lived and that His life radically altered human history forever. Historian Jaroslav Pelikan makes this clear: "Regardless of what anyone may personally think or believe about him, Jesus of Nazareth has been the dominant figure in the history of Western culture for almost twenty centuries. If it were possible, with some sort of supermagnet, to pull up out of that history every scrap of metal bearing at least a trace of his name, how much would be left? It is from his birth that most of the human race dates its calendars, it is by his name that millions curse and in his name that millions pray." (Pelikan, JTTC, 1)

Jesus thought it was fundamentally important what others believed about Him. It was not a subject that allowed for neutrality. C. S. Lewis, a former agnostic, captured this truth in his book *Mere Christianity*. Lewis writes:

> "I am trying here to prevent anyone saying the really foolish thing that people often say about Him: 'I'm ready to accept Jesus as a great moral teacher, but I don't accept His claim to be God.' That is the one thing we must not say. A man who was merely a man and said the sort of things Jesus said would not be a great moral teacher. He would either be a lunatic—on a level with the man who says he is a poached egg—or else he would be the Devil of Hell. You must make your choice.

Either this man was, and is, the Son of God: or else a mad man or something worse. You can shut Him up for a fool, you can spit at Him and kill Him as a demon; or you can fall at His feet and call Him Lord and God. But let us not come up with any patronizing nonsense about His being a great human teacher. He has not left that open to us. He did not intend to" (Lewis, MC'52, 40, 41).

2 A. Three Alternatives

Some people believe Jesus is God because they believe the Bible is inspired by God, and since it teaches that Jesus is God, well then He must be God. Though I too believe that the Bible is the wholly inspired word of God, I do not think one needs to hold that belief in order to arrive at the conclusion that Jesus is God. Here's why:

We have already seen that the New Testament books are historically accurate and reliable; so reliable, in fact, that Jesus cannot be dismissed as a mere legend. The Gospel accounts preserve an accurate record of the things He did, the places He visited, and the words He spoke. And Jesus definitely claimed to be God. Every person must answer the question: Is His claim to deity true or false? This question deserves a serious consideration. If Jesus' claims are true, then He is the Lord, and we must either accept or reject His lordship. We are "without excuse."

If Jesus' claims to be God were false, then

there are just two options: He either knew His claims were false, or He did not know they were false. We will consider each alternative separately and then consider the evidence.

1 B. Was He a Liar?

If, when Jesus made His claims, He knew He was not God, then He was lying. But if He was a liar, then He was also a hypocrite, because He told others to be honest, whatever the cost, while He, at the same time, was teaching and living a colossal lie.

More than that, He was a demon, because He deliberately told others to trust Him for their eternal destiny. If He could not back up His claims and knew they were false, then He was unspeakably evil.

Last, He would also be a fool, because it was His claims to deity that led to His crucifixion.

> Mark 14:61-64: "But He kept silent, and made no answer. Again the high priest was questioning Him, and saying to Him, 'Are You the Christ, the Son of the Blessed One?'
> "And Jesus said, 'I am; and you shall see the Son of Man sitting at the right hand of Power, and coming with the clouds of heaven.'"

If Jesus was a liar, a con man, and therefore an evil, foolish man, then how can we explain the fact that He left us with the most profound moral instruction and powerful moral example that anyone

ever has left? Could a deceiver—an imposter of
monstrous proportions—teach such unselfish ethical
truths and live such a morally exemplary life as Jesus
did? The very notion is incredulous. When the
church historian Philip Schaff considered the evidence for Jesus' deity, especially in light of what Jesus
taught and the kind of life He led, Schaff was struck
by the absurdity of the explanations designed to
escape the logical implications of this evidence.
Stated Schaff:

> This testimony, if not true, must be
> down right blasphemy or madness. The for-
> mer hypothesis cannot stand a moment before
> the moral purity and dignity of Jesus, revealed
> in His every word and work, and acknowledged
> by universal consent. Self-deception in a mat-
> ter so momentous, and with an intellect in all
> respects so clear and so sound, is equally out of
> the question. How could He be an enthusiast
> or a madman who never lost the even balance
> of His mind, who sailed serenely over all the
> troubles and persecutions, as the sun above the
> clouds, who always returned the wisest answer
> to tempting questions, who calmly and delib-
> erately predicted His death on the cross, His
> resurrection on the third day, the outpouring of
> the Holy Spirit, the founding of His Church,
> the destruction of Jerusalem—predictions
> which have been literally fulfilled? A character

so original, so complete, so uniformly consistent, so perfect, so human and yet so high above all human greatness, can be neither a fraud nor a fiction. The poet, as has been well said, would in this case be greater than the hero. It would take more than a Jesus to invent a Jesus. (Schaff, HCC, 109)

The answer, of course, is that Jesus could not have! Someone who lived as Jesus lived, taught as Jesus taught, and died as Jesus died could not have been a liar.

So what are the other alternatives?

2 B. Was He a Lunatic?

If it is inconceivable for Jesus to have been a liar, then could He have thought He was God but have been mistaken? After all, it is possible to be both sincere and wrong.

But we must remember that for someone to think he was God, especially in a culture that was fiercely monotheistic, and then to tell others that their eternal destiny depends on believing in him, was no slight flight of fantasy but the thoughts of a lunatic in the fullest sense. Was Jesus Christ such a person?

Christian philosopher Peter Kreeft presents this option, then shows why we must reject it:

A measure of your insanity is the size of

the gap between what you think you are and what you really are. If I think I am the greatest philosopher in America, I am only an arrogant fool; if I think I am Napoleon, I am probably over the edge . . . But if I think I am God, I am even more insane because the gap between anything finite and the infinite God is even greater than the gap between any two finite things, even a man and a butterfly. Well, then, why [was not Jesus a] liar or lunatic? ... [A]lmost no one who has read the Gospels can honestly and seriously consider that option. The savviness, the canniness, the human wisdom, the attractiveness of Jesus emerge from the Gospels with unavoidable force to any but the most hardened and prejudiced reader.... . Compare Jesus with liars ... or lunatics like the dying Nietzsche. Jesus has in abundance precisely those three qualities that liars and lunatics most conspicuously lack: (1) his practical wisdom, his ability to read human hearts; (2) his deep and winning love, his passionate compassion, his ability to attract people and make them feel at home and forgiven, his authority, "not as the scribes"; (3) his ability to astonish, his unpredictability, his creativity. Liars and lunatics are all so dull and predictable! No one who knows both the Gospels and human beings can seriously entertain the possibility that

Jesus was a liar or a lunatic, a bad man. (Kreeft, FOTF, 60, 61)

The truth is, Jesus was not only sane, but the counsel He provided gives us the most concise and accurate formula for peace of mind and heart.

3 B. He Is Lord!

If Jesus of Nazareth is not a liar or a lunatic, then He must be Lord.

- "Thou art the Christ, the Son of the living God," Peter proclaimed (Matt. 16:18 nasv).
- "My Lord and my God!" Thomas exclaimed after seeing the resurrected Jesus standing before him (John 20:28 NKJV).

Other self-proclaimed gods and saviors have come and gone upon history's stage, but Jesus is still here, standing head-and-shoulders above them all. The modern historian Arnold J. Toynbee spent page after page discussing the exploits of history's so-called "saviours of society"—those who have tried to prevent some social calamity or cultural disintegration by heralding the past, or pointing people toward the future, or waging war or bartering for peace, or claiming wisdom or divinity. After covering such individuals in his magnum opus *Study of History*, Toynbee finally comes to Jesus Christ and finds there is no comparison:

When we first set out on this quest we found ourselves moving in the midst of a mighty marching host; but as we have pressed forward on our way the marchers, company by company, have been falling out of the race. The first to fail were the swordsmen, the next the archaists, the next the futurists, the next the philosophers, until at length there were no more human competitors left in the running. In the last stage of all, our motley host of would-be saviours, human and divine, has dwindled to a single company of none but gods; and now the strain has been testing the staying-power of these last remaining runners, notwithstanding their superhuman strength. At the final ordeal of death, few, even of these would-be saviour-gods, have dared to put their title to the test by plunging into the icy river. And now as we stand and gaze with our eyes fixed upon the farther shore, a single figure rises from the flood, and straightway fills the whole horizon. There is the Saviour; "and the pleasure of the Lord shall prosper in his hand; he shall see of the travail of his soul and shall be satisfied." (Toynbee, SOH, 278)

Who you decide Jesus Christ is must not be an idle intellectual exercise. You cannot put Him on the shelf as a great moral teacher. That is not a valid option. He is either a liar, a lunatic, or the Lord.

You must make a choice. "But," as the apostle John wrote, "these have been written that you may believe that Jesus is the Christ, the Son of God"; and more important, "that believing you may have life in His name" (John 20:31 nasb).

The evidence is clearly in favor of Jesus as Lord. However, some people reject the clear evidence because of the moral implications involved. There needs to be a moral honesty in the above consideration of Jesus as either liar, lunatic, or Lord and God. ☀

JOSH MCDOWELL IS AN INTERNATIONALLY known speaker, author, and traveling representative for Campus Crusade for Christ. A graduate of Wheaton College and Talbot Theological Seminary, he has written more than forty-five books, including the classic *A Ready Defense,* and appeared in numerous films, videos, and televisions series. Josh and his wife Dottie have four children and reside in the Dallas, TX area.

THE NEW EVIDENCE THAT DEMANDS A VERDICT
Hardcover, 800 pages
© 1999 by Josh D. McDowell. A substantial portion of this material was originally published by Here's Life Publishers Inc. © 1972, 1975, 1981 Campus Crusade for Christ Inc.
Thomas Nelson Publishers
ISBN: 0785243631

∽ SPIRITUAL GROWTH ∽
Knowing God
J.I. PACKER

Knowing God *has shown*
readers worldwide the joy
of knowing God. Next to
Scripture, this could be the
most significant book you
will read this year.

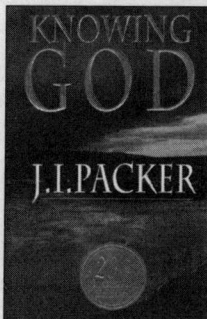

The Study of God

ON JANUARY 7, 1855, THE minister of New Park
Street Chapel, Southwark, England, opened his
morning sermon as follows:

> It has been said by someone that "the
> proper study of mankind is man." . . . I
> believe it is equally true that the proper study
> of God's elect is God; the proper study of a

Christian is the Godhead. The highest science, the loftiest speculation, the mightiest philosophy, which can ever engage the attention of a child of God, is the name, the nature, the person, the work, the doings, and the existence of the great God whom he calls his Father.

There is something exceedingly improving to the mind in a contemplation of the Divinity. It is a subject so vast, that all our thoughts are lost in its immensity; so deep, that our pride is drowned in its infinity. . . .

But while the subject *humbles* the mind, it also expands it. He who often thinks of God, will have a larger mind than the man who simply plods around this narrow globe. . . . The most excellent study for expanding the soul, is the science of Christ, and Him crucified, and the knowledge of the Godhead in the glorious Trinity. Nothing will so enlarge the intellect, nothing so magnify the whole soul of man, as a devout, earnest, continued investigation of the great subject of the Deity.

And whilst humbling and expanding, this subject is eminently *consolatory*. . . . I know nothing which can so comfort the soul; so calm the swelling billows of sorrow and grief; so speak peace to the winds of trial, as a devout musing upon the subject of the Godhead.

These words, spoken over a century ago by C. H. Spurgeon, were true then, and they are true now.

Who Needs Theology?

"But wait a minute," says someone. "In Spurgeon's day, we know, people found theology interesting, but I find it boring. Surely a layperson, at any rate, can get on without it?"

A fair question!—but there is, I think, a convincing answer to it. The questioner clearly assumes that a study of the nature and character of God will be impractical and irrelevant for life. In fact, however, it is the most practical project anyone can engage in. Knowing about God is crucially important for the living of our lives. The world becomes a strange, mad, painful place, and life in it a disappointing and unpleasant business, for those who do not know about God. Disregard the study of God, and you sentence yourself to stumble and blunder through life blindfolded, as it were, with no sense of direction and no understanding of what surrounds you. This way you can waste your life and lose your soul.

Recognizing, then, that the study of God is worthwhile, we prepare to start. But where shall we start from?

Clearly, we can only start from where we are. That, however, means setting out in a storm, for the doctrine of God is a storm center today. We are told that "God-talk," as Christians have historically practiced it, is a refined sort of nonsense, and knowledge about God is strictly a nonentity. Types of teaching which profess such knowledge are written off as outmoded. What are we to do? If we postpone our journey till the storm dies down, we may never get started at all.

My proposal is this. I ask you for the moment to stop your ears to those who tell you there is no road to knowledge about God, and come a little way with me and see. After all, the proof of the pudding is in the eating, and anyone who is actually following a recognized road will not be too worried if he hears nontravelers telling each other that no such road exists.

Storm or no storm, then, we are going to start. But how do we plot our course?

Five basic truths, five foundation principles of the knowledge about God which Christians have, will determine our course throughout.

    1. God has spoken to man, and the Bible is his Word, given to us to make us wise unto salvation.

    2. God is Lord and King over his world; he rules all things for his own glory, displaying his perfections in all that he does, in order that men and angels may worship and adore him.

    3. God is a Savior, active in sovereign love through the Lord Jesus Christ to rescue

believers from the guilt and power of sin, to adopt them as his children and to bless them accordingly.

4. God is triune; there are within the Godhead three persons, the Father, the Son and the Holy Spirit; and the work of salvation is one in which all three act together, the Father purposing redemption, the Son securing it and the Spirit applying it.

5. Godliness means responding to God's revelation in trust and obedience, faith and worship, prayer and praise, submission and service. Life must be seen and lived in the light of God's Word. This, and nothing else, is true religion.

In the light of these general and basic truths, we are in the position of travelers who, after surveying a great mountain from afar, traveling around it, and observing how it dominates the landscape and determines the features of the surrounding countryside, now approach it directly, with the intention of climbing it.

The Basic Themes

What is the ascent going to involve? What are the themes that will occupy us?

We shall have to deal with the *Godhead* of God, the qualities of deity which set God apart from humans and mark the difference and distance between the Creator and his creatures: such qualities as his self-existence, his infinity, his eternity, his unchangeableness. We shall have to deal with the *powers* of God: his almightiness, his omniscience, his omnipresence. We shall have to deal with the *perfections* of God, the aspects of his moral character which are manifested in his words and deeds—his holiness, his love and mercy, his truthfulness, his faithfulness, his goodness, his patience, his justice. We shall have to take note of what pleases him, what offends him, what awakens his wrath, what affords him satisfaction and joy.

For many of us, these are comparatively unfamiliar themes. Few will ever have read anything simple and straightforward on the subject of the nature of God, for scarcely any such writing exists. We can expect, therefore, that an exploration of the themes mentioned above will give us much that is new to think about and many fresh ideas to ponder and digest.

Knowledge Applied

For this very reason we need, before we start to ascend our mountain, to ask ourselves a question that we always ought to put to ourselves whenever we embark on any line of study in God's holy book: What is my ultimate aim and object in occupying my mind with these things? What do I intend to *do* with my knowledge about God, once I have it? For the fact that we have to face is this: If we pursue theological knowledge for its own sake, it is bound to go bad on us. It will make us proud and conceited. The very greatness of the subject matter will intoxicate us, and we shall come to think of ourselves as a cut above other Christians because of our interest in it and grasp of it; and we shall look down on those whose theological ideas seem to us crude and inadequate and dismiss them as very poor specimens. For, as Paul told the conceited Corinthians, "Knowledge puffs up" (I Cor 8:1).

To be preoccupied with getting theological knowledge as an end in itself, to approach Bible study with no higher a motive than a desire to know all the answers, is the direct route to a state of self-satisfied self-deception. We need to guard our hearts against such an attitude, and pray to be kept from it. As we saw earlier, there can be no spiritual health without doctrinal knowledge; But it is equally true that there can be no spiritual health *with* it, if it is sought for the wrong purpose and valued by the wrong standard. In this way, doctrinal study really can become a danger to spiritual life.

"But," says someone, "is it not a fact that a love for God's revealed truth, and a desire to know as much of it as one can, are natural to every person who has been born again?" Look at Psalm 119: "teach me your decrees"; "open my eyes that I may see wonderful things in your law"; "Oh, how I love your law!"; "How sweet are your words to my taste, sweeter than honey to my mouth!"; "give me discernment that I may understand your statutes" (vv. 12, 18, 97, 103, 125). Do not all children of God long, with the psalmist, to know just as much about our heavenly Father as we can learn? Is not, indeed, the fact that we have received a love for his truth in this way one proof that we have been born again? (See 2 Thess 2:10.) And is it not right that we should seek to satisfy this God-given desire to the full?

Yes, of course it is. But if you look back to Psalm 119 again, you will see that the psalmist's concern to get knowledge about God was not a theoretical but a practical concern. He wanted to understand God's truth in order that his heart might respond to it and his life be conformed to it. Observe the emphasis of the opening verses: "Blessed are they whose ways are blameless, who *walk according to the law of the LORD. Blessed are they who keep his statues and seek him with all their heart. . . .* Oh, that my ways were steadfast in *obeying your decrees?*" (vv. 1-2, 5).

This must be our attitude too. Our aim in studying the Godhead must be to know God himself better. As he is the subject of our study, and our helper in it, so he must himself be the end of it. We must seek, in studying God, to be led to God. It was for this purpose that revelation was given, and it is to this use that we must put it.

Meditating on the Truth

How are we to do this? How can we turn our knowledge *about* God into knowledge *of* God? The rule for doing this is simple but demanding: we turn each truth that we learn *about* God into matter for meditation *before* God, leading to prayer and praise *to* God.

We have some idea, perhaps, what prayer is, but what is meditation? Well may we ask, for meditation is a lost art today, and Christian people suffer grievously from their ignorance of the practice.

Meditation is the activity of calling to mind, and thinking over, and dwelling on, and applying to oneself, the various things that one knows about the works and ways and purposes and promises of God. It is an activity of holy thought, consciously performed in the presence of God, under the eye of God, by the help of God, as a means of communion with God.

Its purpose is to clear one's mental and spiritual vision of God, and to let his truth make its full and proper impact on one's mind and heart. It is a matter of talking to oneself about God and oneself; it is, indeed, often a matter of arguing with oneself, reasoning oneself out of moods of doubt and unbelief into a clear apprehension of God's power and grace.

Its effect is ever to humble us, as we contemplate God's greatness and glory and our own littleness and sinfulness, and to encourage and reassure us—"comfort" us, in the old, strong, Bible sense of the word—as we contemplate the unsearchable riches of divine mercy displayed in the Lord Jesus Christ. And it is as we enter more and more deeply into this experience of being humbled and exalted that our knowledge of God increases, and with it our peace, our strength and our joy. God help us, then, to put our knowledge about God to this use, that we all may in truth "know the Lord." ✵

J. I. PACKER IS BOARD OF GOVERNORS Professor of Theology at Regent College in Vancouver, British Columbia. He also serves as a contributing editor to *Christianity Today* and is the author of many books, most recently (with Tom Oden) *One Faith: The Evangelical Consensus.*

KNOWING GOD
Hardcover, 312 pages (includes study guide)
Paper, 286 pages
© 1973 by J.I. Packer
InterVarsity Press
ISBNs: 0-8308-1651-8, hardcover; -1650-X, paper

Knowing God is published in cloth and paper editions in the United States by InterVarsity Press, and in the United Kingdom by Hodder & Stoughton. It is available in cloth and paper formats, with an accompanying study guide that is included in the cloth edition. Canadian customers interested in purchasing the cloth edition should contact InterVarsity Press; those interested in the paper edition should contact Hodder & Stoughton.

⌘ INSPIRATIONAL ⌘

God's Best Secrets

ANDREW MURRAY

Updated in modern English, God's Best Secrets *showcases the insight and beauty of Andrew Murray's original daily devotional readings.*

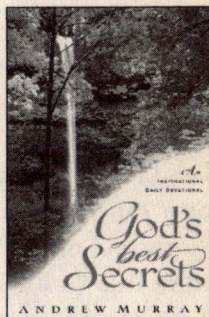

THE MORE I THINK of and pray about the state of religion in this country and all over the world, the deeper my conviction becomes that the low state of the spiritual life of Christians is due to the fact that they do not realize that the aim and object of conversion is to bring the soul, even here on earth, *to a daily fellowship with the Father in heaven.* When once this truth has been accepted, the believer will perceive how indispensable it is to the spiritual life of a Christian to take time each day with God's Word and, in prayer, to wait upon God for His presence and His love to be revealed.

But how can Christians be taught this lesson and live in obedience to it? The first thing is that they must be convinced of the great need of daily fellowship with God. They must be brought under the impression that it is not enough at conversion to accept forgiveness of sins or even to surrender themselves to God. That is only a beginning. The young believer must understand that he has no power of his own to maintain his spiritual life. No, he needs each day to receive new grace from heaven through communion with the Lord Jesus. This cannot be obtained by a hasty prayer or a superficial reading of a few verses from God's Word. He must take time quietly and deliberately to come into God's presence, to feel his weakness and his need, to wait upon God through His Holy Spirit, and to renew the heavenly light and life in his heart. Then he may rightly expect to be kept by the power of Christ throughout the day and all its temptations.

It has been my aim in writing this book to help Christians to see the absolute necessity of communion with the Lord Jesus. Without this the joy and power of God's Holy Spirit in daily life cannot be experienced. Many of God's children long for a better life but do not realize the need of giving God time day by day in their inner chamber for His Spirit to renew and sanctify their lives.

Meditate on this thought: *The feeble state of my spiritual life is mainly due to the lack of time day by day in fellowship with God. New life will dawn in many a soul as a result of time spent in prayer alone with God.*

To any reader who has found a blessing in reading this book—I pray you, share the blessing with others. If you have accepted the message that the Lord Jesus will from day to day grant you His presence and love—pass it on to others. However weak and unworthy you feel, your faith will be strengthened as you help others to realize the need of fellowship with Jesus daily.

As we think of the need of our country and church, as we think of souls around us, as we think of the extension of God's Kingdom, we ask you, O Christians, to help us find volunteers who, as true soldiers of the Cross, will persevere continually in prayer till God pour out His blessing upon us—

Your Servant in the love of Christ and in prayer,

Andrew Murray

January 1

From Day to Day

"The inner man is renewed from day to day"
(2 Cor. 4:16)

There is one lesson that all young Christians should learn, namely this—*the absolute necessity of fellowship with Jesus each day.* This lesson is not always taught at the beginning of the Christian life nor is it always understood by the young convert. He should realize that the grace he has received of the forgiveness of sins, of acceptance as God's child, of joy in the Holy Spirit can only be preserved by the daily renewal in fellowship with Jesus Christ Himself.

Many Christians backslide because this truth is not clearly taught. They are unable to stand against the temptations of the world or of their old nature. They strive to do their best to fight against sin and to serve God, but they have no strength. They have never really grasped the secret: *The Lord Jesus will every day* from heaven continue His work in me. But on one condition—*the soul must give Him time each day* to impart His love and His grace. Time alone with the Lord Jesus each day is the indispensable condition of growth and power.

Read Matthew 11:25–30. Listen to Christ's word: "Come unto Me, and I will give you rest. Learn of Me, and ye shall find rest unto your souls." The Lord will teach us just how meek and humble He is. Bow before Him, tell Him that you long for Him and His love, and He will let His love rest on you. This is a thought not only for young Christians but for all who love the Lord, and this book would gladly help those who desire to live this life of fellowship with Christ. We will try to put the message as clearly, as lovingly, as urgently as possible.

Blessed Father, for Christ's sake and in order to please Him, for my own sake and to enable me to enjoy this blessed experience each day, I will learn the lesson, to **spend time each day**—*without exception*—**in fellowship with Thee.** *So will my soul be renewed from day to day. Amen.*

Fellowship with God

"He that loveth Me shall be loved of my Father.
I will love Him" (John 14:21)

The Three Persons in the Godhead are the Father, the Son, and the Holy Spirit. Each one knows Himself as different from the others. God desires to reveal Himself as a Person. Each one of us is an individual, knowing himself as distinct from others and standing in certain relations to others. God will reveal Himself to us as a Person, and it is our holy calling to enter into fellowship with Him.

God greatly desires this fellowship with man. But sin has come between man and his God. Even in the Christian who thinks he knows God, there is often great ignorance and even indifference to this personal relationship of love to God.

People believe that at conversion their sins are forgiven, that God accepts them so that they may go to heaven, and that they should try to do God's will. But the idea is strange to them that even as a father and his child on earth have pleasure in fellowship, *so they may and must each day have this blessed fellowship with God.*

God gave Christ His Son to bring us to Himself. But this is only possible when we live in close fellowship with Jesus Christ. Our relationship to Christ rests on His deep, tender love to us. We are not able of ourselves to render Him this love. But the Holy Spirit will do the work in us. For this we need to separate ourselves each day from the world and turn in faith to the Lord Jesus, that He may shed abroad His love in our hearts, *so that we may be filled with a great love to Him.*

Dear soul, meditate quietly on this thought. Read the words of Christ in John 14:21, "He that loveth Me shall be loved of my Father. I will love Him." Take time to believe in this personal fellowship. Tell Him of your love.

Blessed Father, Thou hast loved me dearly; most earnestly do I desire to love Thee above all. Amen.

January 3

Jesus

"Thou shalt call His Name Jesus, for He shall save His people from their sins" (Matt. 1:21)

As the Lord Jesus was a person, He had His own individual name. His mother, His disciples, all His friends called Him by this name—Jesus. But they probably thought little of what that name meant. And how little do the majority of Christians know what a treasure is contained in that name—Jesus—*"He shall save His people from their sins."*

Many think of His death on the cross, they think of His work in heaven as Intercessor, but do they, or do we, realize that He is a living Person in heaven who thinks of us each day and longs to reveal Himself? And He desires us each day to bring Him our love and adoration.

Christians pray to Christ to save them from their sins, but they know very little how the blessed work is done. The living Christ reveals Himself to us, and through the power of His love, the love of sin is expelled. It is *through personal fellowship* with Him that Jesus saves us from our sins. I must come as an individual, with my heart and all the sin that is in it, to Jesus as an Almighty personal Savior in whom God's holiness dwells. And as He and I commune together in the expression of mutual love and desire by the work of His Holy Spirit in my heart, His love will expel and conquer all the sin.

O Christian, learn the blessedness of each day in fellowship with Jesus. Finding the secret of happiness and holiness, your heart will long for the hour of prayer as the best hour of the day. As you learn to go apart with Him alone each day, you will experience His presence with you, enabling you all through the day to love Him, to serve Him, and to walk in His ways.

Blessed Father, through this unbroken fellowship with Thee, let me learn the secret of the power of a truly godly life. Amen.

January 4

The Inner Chamber

"When thou prayest enter into thine inner chamber" (Matt.6:6 RV)

Have you ever thought what a wonderful privilege it is that everyone each day and each hour of the day has the liberty of asking God to meet him in the inner chamber and to hear what He has to say? We should imagine that every Christian uses such a privilege gladly and faithfully.

"When thou prayest," says Jesus, "enter into thine inner chamber, and having shut thy door, pray to thy Father which is in secret." That means two things. Shut the world out, withdraw from all worldly thoughts and occupations, and shut yourself in alone with God to pray to Him in secret. Let this be your chief object in prayer, *to realize the presence of your heavenly Father.* Let your watchword be: Alone with God.

This is only the beginning. I must take time to realize His presence with me and pray to my Father who seeth in secret, in the full assurance that He knows how I long for His help and guidance and will incline His ear to me.

Then follows the great promise: "Thy Father which seeth in secret shall reward thee openly." My Father will see to it that my prayer is not in vain. All through the occupations of a busy day, the answer to my prayer will be granted. *Prayer in secret will be followed by the secret working of God in my heart.*

As the Lord Jesus has given us the promise of His presence and shows us the way to the inner chamber, He will assuredly be with us to teach us to pray. It is through Him that we have access to

the Father. Be childlike and trustful in your fellowship with Christ. *Prayer in fellowship* with Jesus
cannot be in vain.

*Blessed Father, I confess each sin, I bring to Thee my every
need. I offer my prayer to Thee in the name of Christ. Amen.* ☆

ANDREW MURRAY (1828–1917) WAS BORN in South Africa,
the son missionaries, and educated in Scotland. He served as
a pastor to established churches and to the thousands of
migrants in Cape colony; he then brought the Keswick
Movement to South Africa. Until his death in 1917, Murray
was considered the father of South African Keswick. He also
spoke extensively at evangelistic meetings in the United States,
Canada, and Great Britain. Murray is known throughout the
English-speaking world for his devotional works, which
include *Abide in Christ* and *With Christ in the School of Prayer.*

GOD'S BEST SECRETS
Paper, 384 pages
© 1993 by Kregel Publications
ISBN: 0-8254-3277-4

Born Again
CHARLES W. COLSON

*Since its initial
publication,* **Born Again**
*has brought hope and
encouragement to millions.
This story of new life
continues to influence
lives around the world.*

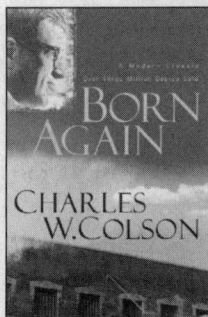

I STOOD THERE WITH my wife, Patty, and son
Wendell, puzzled. This night—election night,
1972—should have been the proudest of my life.
Certainly a Victory Party was called for—the landslide reelection of Richard Nixon to the Presidency
of the United States.

Nothing was amiss about the setting. The

high-ceilinged ornate ballroom of Washington's
Shoreham Hotel was packed with distinguished
gray-suited men, elegant ladies in rich furs. Yet the
picture was out of focus. Something wrong.

I stood there thinking that, unlike any celebration I had attended in twenty years in politics,
there was no air of triumph here. The faces before
us were unsmiling, looking, in fact, disappointed
and even imposed upon. Around the big boards
where the continuing returns were posting record-
breaking margins for Nixon, there was scarcely a
ripple of excitement.

My mind went back to the comparable scene
four years before at the Waldorf in New York. What
a contrast! That 1968 Victory Party had been alive,
high drama indeed. I recalled the scene so vividly—
the Waldorf ballroom jammed with eager young
people who had worked so hard for months to oust
the Democrats. All that long night as the brass ring
neared their grasp, the excitement mounted until
the sweet smell of victory filled the air. As the vote
count on the big boards edged up, precinct by
precinct, how they *ooh*ed and sighed and laughed
and slapped one another on the back and roared
their approval.

But tonight?

Patty turned to me. "What's wrong, Chuck?
You're so quiet."

"I don't *know* what's wrong. Just exhausted, I
guess." With a nod and a gesture I indicated the

throng pushing and shoving four deep around the bar. "The only thing these people seem to care about is the free booze."

"Let's walk around," Wendell suggested. "See what people are saying." In only two weeks as a campaign volunteer, Wendell had learned a lot. Now he sought further insights to take back to his political-science course at Princeton.

And I wanted insights, too.

In the VIP area the comments were griping ones. . . . Where was Nixon? Shouldn't their $25,000 contributions entitle them to at least a handshake on election night? Then we were cornered by Senator Bob Dole, the Republican national chairman. Angrily he jabbed his finger at me: "The President didn't even mention the Committee in his speech."

After that a group of dour-faced party hangers-on surrounded us. "I want to see you about my job," one old stalwart said unsmilingly as he clutched my arm. None of the other senior White House staffers were there, and in minutes I was being swamped with requests.

No, I wasn't imagining the sour mood. But something was also wrong in me. My insides were as deadened as the air in the room and the slow beat of the music. My lack of exhilaration made no sense. Being part of electing a President was the fondest ambition of my life. For three long years I had committed everything I had, every ounce of energy to

Richard Nixon's cause. Nothing else had mattered. We had had no time together as a family, no social life, no vacations. So why could my tongue not taste the flavor of this hour of conquest?

Just then my little beeper, the radio receiver which I snapped to my belt whenever I was out of telephone reach, went off. There was a shrill whistle. Then as I lifted the gadget to my ear, came the command, "Colson, Colson, report to the White House operator."

It was the President. He wanted me at once in his office, the operator said when I called in. A limousine sped Patty, Wendell, and me through the darkness, past nearly deserted Rock Creek Park, to downtown Washington, and at last through the iron gates to the White House grounds.

A blue-suited officer, his braid glittering in the glow of floodlights, snapped a salute and told me that Mr. Nixon was in his "working" office in the Executive Office Building, called the E.O.B. Nixon used the traditional Oval Office in the west wing of the White House chiefly for formal meetings, preferring to work in the quiet intimacy of the denlike office in the E.O.B. across the alleyway. This mammoth gray Victorian structure bristling with gingerbread, arches, and turrets had one held the entire State and War Departments, but now house only the White House staff.

When we got there we found one lone Secret Service agent in the marble-floored hallway. He waved us in and watched while I deposited Patty and Wendell in my office next to the President's. "I'll only be a few minutes," I told them. "Then we'll go home to bed."

Back in the darkened hall, the Secret Service agent spoke softly: "He's waiting for you, Mr. Colson." I swung open the ten-foot-high door to find Richard Nixon reclining in his favorite easy chair, smiling and puffing contentedly on his pipe. The President was wearing the light-blue checked sport jacket he always slipped on when in the privacy of his office and I blinked a little at the eye-blurring combination of blue checks with the dark blue pinstripe of his trousers.

A few feet away Bob Haldeman, Nixon's chief of staff, was sitting at a small antique table poring over election returns. His back was to the door and he never looked up as I walked in.

The President greeted me with a big grin and, "Good job, boy, good job." Haldeman still did not look up.

"Sit down, Chuck, and have a drink with me," he said. The President rang for Manola, his Cuban valet, who scurried in with two Scotch and sodas.

Haldeman never drank, and I imagined Nixon had been anxiously awaiting my arrival. "Here's to you, Chuck. Those are *your* votes that are pouring in, the Catholics, the union members, the blue-collars, your votes, boy. It was your strategy and it's a landslide!" Nixon lifted his glass to me and then gulped almost half its contents in one swallow.

"The way the votes are piling up, you are going to top sixty-one percent, Mr. President. That's a record," I said and then reminded him of a modest bet we'd made the day before.

Haldeman was still busy totaling up numbers, once snatching the phone beside him to berate his young assistant, Larry Higby, for not providing the latest figures. Watching Bob's scowling face, I saw a replay of the faces at the Shoreham. From Bob's attitude, I could have thought we were losing the election.

"Bob and I were just talking before you came in, Chuck," the President rambled on. "It was ten years ago almost to the day that they wrote us off. We were 'dead' in California, finished, all through. Look at us now—on top—biggest vote ever," he chortled. "I guess we showed 'em! Right?" He smacked a fist into his outstretched palm.

Nixon drank again, emptying his glass, then went into the large lavatory off the far side of the room. I turned to the grim-lipped Haldeman. "What's eating you?"

Bob's eyes, blue and steely cold darted up from his papers, meeting mine for the first time, a deep frown on his forehead. His short crew cut seemed to bristle, too. "I'm trying to add the actual figures—don't be giving him your guesses," he snapped.

Haldeman, I assumed, was tired. Perhaps he

was also resenting the fact that I was sharing this moment of victory with the President. Of course there were always petty jealousies in the White House.

"What's wrong, Chuck? Why aren't you smiling and celebrating?" Nixon asked, returning to his chair.

"I guess I'm a bit numb, sir."

"This is a night to remember. Have another drink. Let's enjoy this." I had always followed Nixon's orders, but you can't order somebody to be happy.

The President then began composing one draft after another of a telegram to send to his vanquished opponent, Senator George McGovern. It was now close to two in the morning. McGovern had conceded hours earlier. By the rules of the game Nixon's response was long overdue. Yet as fast as the words rolled off his tongue, he would reject them. "How can I say something nice after he kept comparing me to Hitler?"

Haldeman handed him a draft written by another aide. Nixon scanned it. "No, I won't say that." He flung the sheet of paper across the little table between Haldeman and myself.

That he could show no charity in this hour of his greatest triumph dramatized the paradox of Richard Nixon. In 1960 evidence suggested that the cliff-hanger election had been stolen from him. "Demand a recount," his aides urged. But Nixon had refused: it would create uncertainty, be bad for the country, and it was his job to help unite the electorate behind the man who defeated him. Noble in defeat, he was now without grace in victory.

Time and again I had seen the President show rare courage when others around him shrank in fear. For this he had won my deepest admiration. Since I had come to respect the President for what he was in his best moments, I learned to accept him for what he was in his worst. I suppose loyalty, like love, creates its own image of what we see.

If someone had peered in on us that night from some imaginary peephole in the ceiling of the President's office, what a curious sight it would have been: a victorious President, grumbling over words he would grudgingly say to his fallen foe; his chief of staff angry, surly, and snarling; and the architect of his political strategy sitting in a numbed stupor. Yes, the picture was out of focus. If this was victory, what might these three men have looked like in defeat?

Nixon told Manola to find us something to eat. That meant waking up a couple of the White House stewards. Shortly before 3:00 a.m. they appeared, sleepy-eyed, carrying three plates of fried eggs and ham. I wished that they had brought some food for Patty and Wendell next door, but decided not to trouble the tired stewards further. The President was chattering on about one Senate race after another, on such a reminiscing kick that we could easily be there until dawn. How could I rescue

Patty and Wendell?

The answer came in a report from Haldeman's assistant; both the Associated Press and United Press wire services had shut down for the night; there would be no more vote totals until morning. That welcome news plus my drooping eyelids must have convinced the President to call it a night.

As we were leaving, Mr. Nixon paused at the top of the long flight of gray cement steps leading to the driveway. Directly in front of us the chalk-white mansion rose up majestically in the darkness. "Chuck," he said, "I just want you to know—I'll always be . . . ."

Knowing how hard it always was for him to show emotions, I interrupted. "Thank you, Mr. President. Tomorrow will be a good day."

With that he turned and started down the steps, with the Secret Service agent in front of him, glancing mechanically from side to side. I stood for a moment, watching the Thirty-seventh President of the United States, now with the greatest mandate in history by which to govern, slowly descending before me. Lights still burning in a few windows cast an orange glow over the green shrubs and velvety lawns. The night air was clear. In the background rose the Washington Monument, tall and proud, a sight which had never ceased to thrill me. But tonight not even this could penetrate the deadness inside me. . . . ✳

CHARLES W. COLSON, FORMER SPECIAL counsel to President Richard Nixon, is the author of 23 books, which have sold more than 5 million copies. In 1976 Colson founded Prison Fellowship, which has since become the world's largest outreach to prisoners, ex-prisoners, and their families. In 1991 he launched *BreakPoint,* a daily radio feature bringing Christian thinking to bear on current issues, which airs on some 1,000 stations nationwide.

BORN AGAIN
Paper, 352 pages
© 1976, 1977, 1995 by Charles W. Colson
Chosen Books, a division of Baker Publishing Group
ISBN: 0-8007-9377-3

~ SPIRITUAL GROWTH ~

Celebration of Discipline

RICHARD J. FOSTER

Celebration of Discipline *has helped more than a million Christian seekers discover a richer spiritual life infused with joy, peace, and a deeper understanding of God.*

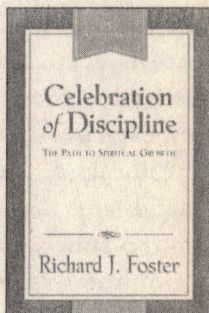

SUPERFICIALITY IS THE CURSE of our age. The doctrine of instant satisfaction is a primary spiritual problem. The desperate need today is not for a greater number of intelligent people, or gifted people, but for deep people.

The classical Disciplines of the spiritual life call us to move beyond surface living into the depths. They invite us to explore the inner caverns of the spiritual realm. They urge us to be the answer to a hollow world. John Woolman counsels, "It is good for thee to dwell deep, that thou mayest feel and understand the spirits of people."

We must not be led to believe that the Disciplines are only for spiritual giants and hence beyond our reach, or only for contemplatives who devote all their time to prayer and mediation. Far from it. God intends the Disciplines of the spiritual life to be for ordinary human beings: people who have jobs, who care for children, who wash dishes and mow lawns. In fact, the Disciplines are best exercised in the midst of our relationships with our husband or wife, our brothers and sisters, our friends and neighbors.

Neither should we think of the Spiritual Disciplines as some dull drudgery aimed at exterminating laughter from the face of the earth. Joy is the keynote of all the Disciplines. The purpose of the Disciplines is liberation from the stifling slavery to self-interest and fear. When the inner spirit is liberated from all that weighs it down, it can hardly be described as dull drudgery. Singing, dancing, even shouting characterize the Disciplines of the spiritual life.

In one important sense, the Spiritual Disciplines are not hard. We need not be well advanced in matters of theology to practice the Disciplines. Recent converts—for that matter people how have yet to turn their lives over to Jesus Christ—can and should practice them. The primary requirement is a longing after God. "As a hart longs for flowing streams, so longs my soul for thee, O God. My soul thirsts for God for the Living God," writes the psalmist.

Beginners are welcome. I, too, am a beginner, even and *especially* after a number of years of practicing every Discipline discussed in this book. As Thomas Merton says, "We do not want to be beginners. But let us be convinced of the fact that we will never be anything else but beginners, all our life!"

Psalm 42:7 reads "Deep calls to deep." Perhaps somewhere in the subterranean chambers of your life you have heard the call to deeper, fuller living. You have become weary of frothy experiences and shallow teaching. Every now and then you have caught glimpses, hints of something more than you have known. Inwardly you long to launch out into the deep.

Those who have heard the distant call deep within and who desire to explore the world of the Spiritual Disciplines are immediately faced with two difficulties. The first is philosophic. The materialistic base of our age has become so pervasive that it has given people grave doubts about their ability to reach beyond the physical world. Many first-rate scientists have passed beyond such doubts, knowing that we cannot be confined to a space-time box. But the average person is influenced by popular science, which is a generation behind the times and is prejudiced against the nonmaterial world.

It is hard to overstate how saturated we are with the mentality of popular science. Meditation, for example, if allowed at all, is not thought of as an encounter between a person and God, but as psychological manipulation. Usually people will tolerate a brief dabbling in the "inward journey," but then it is time to get on with *real* business in the *real* world. We need the courage to move beyond the prejudice of our age and affirm with our best scientists that more than the material world exists. In intellectual honesty, we should be willing to study and explore the spiritual life with all the rigor and determination we would give to any field of research.

The second difficulty is a practical one. We simply do not know how to go about exploring the inward life. This has not always been true. In the first century and earlier, it was not necessary to give instruction on how to "do" the Disciplines of the spiritual life. The Bible called people to such Disciplines as fasting, prayer, worship, and celebration but gave almost no instruction about how to do them. The reason for this is easy to see. Those Disciplines were so frequently practiced and such a part of the general culture that the "how to" was common knowledge. Fasting, for example, was so common that no one had to ask what to eat before a fast, or how to break a fast, or how to avoid dizziness while fasting—everyone already knew.

This is not true of our generation. Today there is an abysmal ignorance of the most simple and practical aspects of nearly all the classic Spiritual Disciplines. Hence, any book written on the subject must provide practical instruction on precisely how we do the Disciplines. One word of caution, however, must be given at the outset: to know the mechanics does not mean that we are practicing the Disciplines. The Spiritual Disciplines are an inward and spiritual reality, and the inner attitude of the heart is far more crucial than the mechanics for coming into the reality of the spiritual life.

In our enthusiasm to practice the Disciplines, we may fail to practice our discipline. The life that is pleasing to God is not a series of religious duties. We have only one thing to do, namely, to experience a life of relationship and intimacy with God, "the Father of lights with whom there is no variation or shadow due to change" (James 1:17).

The Slavery of Ingrained Habits

We are accustomed to thinking of sin as individual acts of disobedience to God. This is true enough as far as it goes, but Scripture goes much further. In Romans the apostle Paul frequently refers to sin as a condition that plagues the human race (i.e., Rom. 3:9-18). Sin as a condition works

its way out through the "bodily members," that is,
the ingrained habits of the body (Rom. 7:5ff). And
there is no slavery that can compare to the slavery of
ingrained habits of sin.

Isaiah 57:20 says, "The wicked are like the
tossing sea; for it cannot rest, and its waters toss up
mire and dirt." The sea does not need to do anything special to produce mire and dirt; that is the
result of its natural motions. This is also true of us
when we are under the condition of sin. The natural motions of our lives produce mire and dirt. Sin
is part of the internal structure of our lives. No
special effort is needed to produce it. No wonder
we feel trapped.

Our ordinary method of dealing with our
ingrained sin is to launch a frontal attack. We rely
on our willpower and determination. Whatever
may be the issue for us—anger, fear, bitterness,
gluttony, pride, lust, substance abuse—we determine never to do it again; we pray against it, fight
against it, set our will against it. But the struggle is
all in vain, and we find ourselves once again morally bankrupt or, worse yet, so proud of our external
righteousness that "whitened sepulchers" is a mild
description of our condition. In his excellent little
book entitled *Freedom from Sinful Thoughts* Heini Arnold
writes, "We...want to make it quite clear that we
cannot free and purify our own heart by exerting
our own 'will.'"

In Colossians Paul lists some of the outward

forms that people use to control sin: "touch not, taste not, handle not." He then adds that these things "have indeed a show of wisdom in *will worship*" (Col. 2:20-23, KJV, [italics added]). "Will worship"—what a telling phrase, and how descriptive of so much of our lives! The moment we feel we can succeed and attain victory over sin by the strength of our will alone is the moment we are worshiping the will. Isn't it ironic that Paul looks at our most strenuous efforts in the spiritual walk and calls them idolatry, "will worship"?

Willpower will never succeed in dealing with the deeply ingrained habits of sin. Emmet Fox writes, "As soon as you resist mentally any undesirable or unwanted circumstance, you thereby endow it with more power—power which it will use against you, and you will have depleted your own resources to that exact extent." Heini Arnold concludes, "As long as we think we can save ourselves by our own will power, we will only make the evil in us stronger than ever." This same truth has been experienced by all the great writers of the devotional life from St. Augustine to St. Francis, from John Calvin to John Wesley, from Teresa of Avila to Julian of Norwich.

"Will worship" may produce an outward show of success for a time, but in the cracks and crevices of our lives our deep inner condition will eventually be revealed. Jesus describes this condition when he speaks of the external righteousness of the Pharisees. "Out of the abundance of the heart the mouth speaks...I tell you, on the day of judgment men will render account for every *careless word* they utter" (Matt. 12:34-36, [italics added]). You see, by dint of will people can make a good showing for a time, but sooner or later there will come that unguarded moment when the "careless word" will slip out to reveal the true condition of the heart. If we are full of compassion, it will be revealed; if we are full of bitterness, that also will be revealed.

It is not that we plan to be this way. We have no intention of exploding with anger or of parading a sticky arrogance, but when we are with people, what we *are* comes out. Though we may try with all our might to hide these things, we are betrayed by our eyes, our tongue, our chin, our hands, our whole body language. Willpower has no defense against the careless word, the unguarded moment. The will has the same deficiency as the law—it can deal only with externals. It is incapable of bringing about the necessary transformation of the inner spirit.

As we enter the inner world of the Spiritual Disciplines, there will always be the danger of turning them into laws. But we are not left to our own human devices. Jesus Christ has promised to be our ever-present Teacher and Guide. His voice is not hard to hear. His direction is not hard to understand. If we are beginning to calcify what should always remain alive and growing, he will tell us. We can trust his teaching. If we are wandering off toward some wrong idea or unprofitable practice, he will guide us back. If we are willing to listen to the Heavenly Monitor, we will receive the instruction we need.

Our world is hungry for genuinely changed people. Leo Tolstoy observes, "Everybody thinks of changing humanity and nobody thinks of changing himself." Let us be among those who believe that the inner transformation of our lives is a goal worthy of our best effort. ☼

———————

RICHARD J. FOSTER IS THE AUTHOR of several top-selling books, including *Streams of Living Water, Freedom of Simplicity* and *Prayer,* which won an ECPA Gold Medallion Award. *Celebration of Discipline,* which has sold over 1 million copies, has been hailed by many as the best modern book on Christian spirituality and described by *Christianity Today* as one of the best 10 books of the 20th century. Foster is the founder of Renovaré, an infrachurch movement committed to the renewal of the church in all her multifaceted expressions and a general editor of the forthcoming *Renovaré Spiritual Formation Study Bible.*

CELEBRATION OF DISCIPLINE
Cloth, 236 pages
© 1978, 1988, 1998 by Richard J. Foster
All rights reserved. Reprinted here by permission from HarperSanFrancisco, a Division of HarperCollins Publishers.
ISBN: 60628391

∽ PRAYER ∽

Practicing His Presence

BROTHER LAWRENCE AND FRANK LAUBACH

*In every century only
a few so earnestly
pursue Jesus. But
there are always a few
who keep lit the
pathway for those who
come after them.*

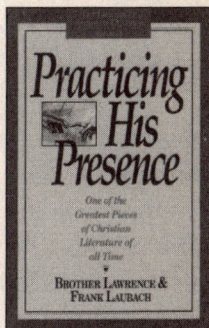

THIS IS THE FIRST CHAPTER by Brother Lawrence from *Practicing His Presence*.

Conversation with a friend August 3, 1666

God did me a glorious favor in bringing me to a conversion at the age of eighteen.

In the winter I saw a tree stripped of its and I

knew that within a little time the leaves would be renewed, and that afterwards the flowers and the fruit
would appear. From this I received a high view of
the power and providence of God which has never
since departed from my soul. The view I grasped
that day set me completely loose from the world and
kindled in me such a love for God that I cannot tell
whether it has increased during the more than forty
years since that time.

I was a footman to M. Fieubert, the treasurer,
but I am a very awkward fellow and seemed to break
everything.

I decided, instead of continuing as a footman, to be received into a monastery. I thought that
perhaps there I would be made, in some way, to suffer for my awkwardness and for all the faults I had
committed. I decided to sacrifice my life with all its
pleasures to God. But He greatly disappointed me
in this idea, for I have met with nothing but satisfaction in giving my life over to Him.

I have found that we can establish ourselves in
a sense of the presence of God by continually talking with Him. It is simply a shameful thing to quit
conversing with Him to think of trifles and foolish
things. We should feed and nourish our souls with
high notions of God which will yield great joy.

We ought to quicken, that is, enliven our
faith. It is lamentable that we have so little faith.
Men amuse themselves with trivial devotions which
change daily instead of making faith in God the rule

of their conduct. The way of faith is the spirit of the church and it is sufficient to bring us to a very high degree of perfection.

We ought to give ourselves up to God in things that are temporal as well as in things that are spiritual. We should seek our satisfaction only in fulfilling His will. If He leads us into suffering or if He leads us into comfort, our satisfaction should still only be for the fulfilling of His will, for both suffering and comfort are the same to a soul truly resigned to Him.

There are times in prayer when God tries our love for Him. In these times of dryness and unclearness which bother our souls, there needs to be fidelity to Him. This is the time for us to make an effectual act of resignation. This will oftentimes increase our spiritual advancement.

Just say, "Lord I am yours, dryness does not matter nor affect me!"

To arrive at the resignation God requires, we should watch attentively over all our passions. These passions mingle as much in spiritual things as in things of a more gross nature. God will give light about these passions to anyone who truly desires to serve Him.

If that is your desire, to sincerely serve God, you may feel free to come to me as often as you please without fear of being troublesome. But if you do not have this as your sincere desire there is no necessity of your visiting with me again.

This is the first chapter by Frank Laubach in *Practicing His Presence.*

January 3, 1930

To be able to look backward and say, "This has been the finest year of my life"—that is glorious! But anticipation! To be able to look ahead and say, "The present year can and shall be better!"—that is more glorious!

If we said such things about our achievements, we would be consummate egotists. But if we are speaking of God's kindness, and we speak truly, we are but grateful. And this is what I do witness. I have done nothing but open windows—*God has done all the rest.* There have been few if any conspicuous achievements. There has been a succession of marvelous experiences of the presence of God. I feel, as I look back over the year, that it would have been impossible to have held much more without breaking with sheer joy. It was the lonesomest year, in some ways the hardest year, of my life, but the most glorious, full of voices from heaven.

As for me, I resolved that I would succeed better this year with my experiment of filling *every minute full of the thought of God than I succeeded last year.*

January 20, 1930

Although I have been a minister and a missionary for fifteen years, I have not lived the entire day of every day, minute by minute to follow the will of God. Two years ago a profound dissatisfaction led me to begin trying to line up my actions with the will of God about every fifteen minutes or every half hour. Other people to whom I confessed this intention said it was impossible. I judge from what I have heard that few people are really trying even that. But this year I have started out to live all my waking moments in conscious listening to the inner voice, asking without ceasing, "What, Father, do you desire said? What Father, do you desire this minute?"

It is clear that this is exactly what Jesus was doing all day every day.

January 26, 1930

For the past few days I have been experimenting in a more complete surrender than ever before. I am taking by deliberate act of will, enough time from each hour to give God much thought. Yesterday and today I have made a new adventure, which is not easy to express. I am feeling God in each movement, by an act of will—willing that He shall direct these fingers that now strike this typewriter—willing that He shall pour through my steps as I walk—willing that He shall direct my words as I speak, and my very jaws as I eat! You will object to this intense introspection. Do not try it, unless you feel dissatisfied with your own relationship with the

Lord, but at least allow me to realize all the
leadership of God I can. Paul speaks of our liberty in Christ. I am trying to be utterly free from
everybody, free from my own self, but completely enslaved to the will of God every moment
of this day.

We used to sing a song in the church in
Benton which I like, but which I never really practiced until now. It runs:

"Moment by moment I'm kept in His love;
Moment by moment I've life from above;
Looking to Jesus till glory doth shine;
Moment by moment, O Lord, I am Thine."

It is exactly that "moment by moment," every
waking moment, surrender, responsiveness, obedience, sensitiveness, pliability, "lost in His love," that
I now have the mind-bent to explore with all my
might, to respond to Jesus Christ as a violin
responds to the bow of the master.

In defense of my opening my soul and laying it bare to the public gaze in this fashion, I may
say that it seems to me that we really seldom do
anybody much good excepting as we share the
deepest experiences of our souls in this way. It is
not the fashion to tell your inmost thoughts, but
there are many wrong fashions, and concealment
of the *best in us is wrong.* I disapprove of the usual
practice of talking "small talk" whenever we meet,

and holding a veil over our souls. If we are so impoverished that we have nothing to reveal but small talk, then we need to struggle for more richness of soul. As for me, I am convinced that this spiritual pilgrimage, which I am making, is infinitely worthwhile, the most important thing I know of to talk about. And talk I shall while there is anybody to listen.

Outside the window, as I completed the last page, has been one of the most splendorous sunsets I have ever seen. And these words came singing through my soul, "Looking to Jesus 'till glory doth shine!" Open your soul and entertain the glory of God and after a while that glory will be reflected in the world about you and in the very clouds above your head.

❖ ❖ ❖

We hope you enjoyed reading the first chapters of *Practicing His Presence*. This is a most practical book on experiencing the depths and riches of Jesus Christ. Below are the remaining chapter titles to encourage you to pursue the *presence of God*.

BROTHER LAWRENCE WAS BORN NICHOLAS Herman in French Lorraine in 1611. He was converted to Christ at the age of 18. In 1666, he entered a religious community called the Carmelites. There he took the name Brother Lawrence and practiced the presence of God while working in the kitchen.

FRANK LAUBACH WAS BORN IN 1884. As a missionary in the

Philippines, he began the practice of abiding in the presence of Christ. By the time of his death in 1970, he was known in virtually every land on earth. He wrote over 50 books and was perhaps the greatest single educator of modern times.

PRACTICING HIS PRESENCE
Paper, 110 pages
© SeedSowers Publishing House
ISBN: 0-940232-01-4

∽ B I O G R A P H Y ∾

Shadow of the Almighty

ELISABETH ELLIOT

The story of Jim Elliot's life and martyrdom is one of the great missionary stories of modern times— and is a modern Christian classic.

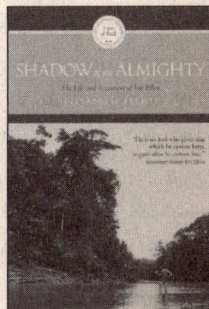

PREFACE

It is only when we obey God's laws that we can be quite sure that we really know Him. The man who claims to know God but does not obey His laws is not only a liar, he lives in self-delusion. In practice, the more a man learns to obey God's law, the more truly and fully does he express his love for Him. Obedience is the test of whether we really live "in God" or not.

*The life of a man who professes to be living in God must bear
the stamp of Christ.*

These words, written about A.D. 90 in the
first epistle of John, embody the radicals of Jim
Elliot's life. Obedience leads to knowledge.
Obedience is the expression of love to God.
Obedience means that we live in God. And if we live
in Him, our lives bear the stamp of Christ.

Some who pick up this book may make no
claim to know God. Others may make the claim but
be victims of the self-delusion that John observes.
Yet others may know Him, and obey Him, but wonder sometimes at the value of this knowledge and
this obedience. I think that this book will have
something to say to all three. If those in the first category want to know God, they may perhaps learn
how. Those in the second group may find that they
are missing a great deal by not backing their claims
with action. And those in the third category may be
encouraged to pursue their course.

Jim's aim was to know God. His course, obedience—the only course that could lead to the
fulfillment of his aim. His end was what some would
call an extraordinary death, although in facing
death he had quietly pointed out that many have
died because of obedience to God.

He and the other men with whom he died
were hailed as heroes, "martyrs." I do not approve.
Nor would they have approved.

Is the distinction between living for Christ and dying for Him, after all, so great? Is not the second the logical conclusion of the first? Furthermore, to live for God *is* to die, "daily," as the apostle Paul put it. It is to lose everything that we may gain Christ. It is in thus laying down our lives that we find them.

The relationship between man and God is a very practical one. It finds its sphere of operation in the common life. Let us not forget that any relationship whatever between God and man rests today on the fact that God lived the life of a common man—was born in a stable, sweated in a carpenter shop, preached from a little fishing boat, sat down tired beside a well and conversed with a courtesan, ate and drank and walked with ordinary men, and submitted to an ignoble death—in order that we could recognize Him. Nobody called Him a hero or a martyr. He was simply doing what His Father told Him to do, and doing it with *delight.*

Those who want to know Him must walk the same path with Him. *These* are the "martyrs" in the Scriptural sense of the word, which means simply "witnesses." In life, as well as in death, we are called to be "witnesses"—to "bear the stamp of Christ."

I believe that Jim Elliot was one of these. His letters and journals are the tangible ground for my belief. They are not mine to withhold. They are a part of the human story, the story of a man in his relation to the Almighty. They are facts.

"I write like I talk—without thinking much beforehand—and sometimes spiel stuff that were better left in the ink bottle," Jim wrote to me in 1948. "I think it was Browning who, having been queried on something he wrote in early life said, 'When I wrote that, two people knew what it meant, God and I. Now only God knows.' So with anything perplexing, throw it out, discounted as an abortion sprung from a mind that is at times overproductive to its own hurt."

Once in 1952 I mentioned to Jim that I had sent an excerpt from one of his letters to a friend. He replied:

"I'm not too excited about your sending my letters to others. I don't like to write a page knowing that perhaps a not-as-sympathetic reader as yourself may scan it. This is a confession that I am not trying to impress you with my letters. I barely reread them, pay little attention to grammar and punctuation, and know that my handwriting has suffered. I guess I will have to trust you to be choosy in sending representations of me to folks whose impression-factors should be delicately censored."

In the task of selection I have not "delicately censored" anything at all which I felt would contribute to the faithful portrayal of the whole man as I knew him. The reader will notice the repetition of certain ideas throughout his writings. He will also wonder if perhaps in certain chapters I have included only those portions of his writings which indicate the growth of his soul, to the exclusion of those which would show a more "human" side of his personality. Of both of these—the repetition, the long passages dealing with soul-exercise—I would say this: I have taken pains to let my choices represent the tone of Jim's writings as a whole, so that the number of excerpts on a given subject, or during a given period, are in direct proportion to the total content of the letters and diaries. There were periods when his writing was occupied almost exclusively with the metaphysical. There were others when it dealt with the mundane.

When Jim was twenty years old he prayed, "Lord make my way prosperous, not that I achieve high station, but that my life may be an exhibit to the value of knowing God." His life was that to me, who shared it more intimately than any other. Was it extraordinary? I offer these pages so that the reader may decide for himself. If his answer is yes— if he finds herein the "stamp of Christ," and decides that this is extraordinary—what shall we shay of the state of Christendom?

INTRODUCTION

At dinner recently with a group of Christian high school and college students, I asked whether they had any heroes. There was silence. They looked at each other, then looked blankly back at me. Heroes? What is a hero?

I was taken aback. While they discussed

definitions I remembered what a long list of heroes
I had when I was their age. I would have had no difficulty in answering the question I had asked, nor
would it have been necessary to define the word.
Gideon, David, Daniel, Shadrach, Meshach, and
Abednego, Hans the Hero of Harlem, Florence
Nightingale, and Abraham Lincoln were on my list,
along with a good many nineteenth- and twentieth-
century missionaries.

No, was the answer of my dinner companions. They had no heroes.

Is there anyone, then, whom you admire?

A short pause, then, hesitantly, well, yes—
some rock stars, a few athletes—people not by any
means always exemplary in many ways, but they had
a goal they worked hard for.

Feeling very sorry for these young people, and
a bit desperate, I asked if there was anyone they
wanted to be like. The answer was an immediate and
definite no. They wanted to do their own thing, be
their own person. That seems to me a hard assign-
ment. If we are to find the channel and the harbor,
surely we need some lights to steer by.

I thought of the words of Hebrews 13:7,
"Remember your leaders, those who first spoke
God's message to you; and reflecting upon the outcome of their life and work, follow the example of
their faith." Many people had spoken God's message to me in many different ways, my parents being
the first. Daily they taught us to pray, to sing hymns,

to read the Bible. Daily they set before us an example of faith. We were not aware of it then, but certainly they were the lights we steered by.

My next door neighbor, Ruth Richie, was another. To a ten-year-old girl, this fifteen-year-old was something of a goddess. She was first of all a "grown-up" to me. She was also pretty, soft-spoken, feminine, and uncommonly kind to the shy and uncertain child next door. She was my heroine. I admired everything about her, wanted to do my hair like hers, and walk like her, talk like her, *be* like her.

When I was twelve-years-old my Sunday School teacher was a lovely young woman named Jane White. Her patience with us giddy adolescents never gave out, so far as I remember (and she went on to complete fifty-four years of teaching junior and senior high school girls). She invited us to her wedding and after to a little party, the first she gave in her home as new bide. I loved the way she had arranged her tiny apartment. I loved her clothes. To me she was perfection.

We entertained scores of missionaries in our home, and in high school and college I began to read missionary biographies. The lives of Hudson Taylor, David Brainerd, John and Betty Stam, and Amy Carmichael deeply molded my desires and aspirations. They became, like those others I knew personally, my models.

I do not think I exaggerate when I say hundreds of young men have told me that *Shadow of the*

Almighty has had a more powerful influence in their lives than any book outside of the Bible. They do not usually use the word *hero.* But in every other way they can express it, they tell me that Jim Elliot has been—well, an *influence.* Many say a role model. Some have said, "That book has changed my life."

Let this be a warning. You can't be too careful what you read. This man's story might do three things:

1. Give you someone to imitate—not a model of perfection by any means, but a man of "like passions" with the rest of us, whose heart was set on God.

2. Show you the pattern of God's sovereign love in the twenty-eight years of a real flesh-and-blood man of our century.

3. Demonstrate that obedience is costly, but the rewards of obedience are priceless— among the few things we *cannot lose.*

I think of the young detective in Belfast who told me of the fear he felt as he went daily into the bombed and barbwired zone of that city, not knowing whether he might at any moment be shot or knee-capped.

"I have a wife and little children," he said, "and I'm sacred—for them. But someone gave me *Shadow of the Almighty.* I read it at night when I went to bed, crying and praying my way through it (it took me a long time!). But it strengthened my faith. 'If

Jim Elliot could go into danger for God, so can I.'
I said."

It is my prayer that many with ears to hear will
reflect on the outcome of Jim's life and work and
follow the example of his faith.

ELISABETH ELLIOT
Magnolia, Massachusetts
October, 1988

PROLOGUE

When Jim was a college student in 1949 he
wrote these words: *"He is no fool who gives what he cannot
keep to gain what he cannot lose."*

Seven years later, on a hot Sunday afternoon,
far from the dormitory room where those lines were
written, he and four other young men were finish-
ing a dinner of baked beans and carrot sticks. They
sat together on a strip of white sand on the Curaray
River, deep in the Ecuador's rain forest, waiting for
the arrival of a group of men whom they loved, but
had never met—savage Stone Age killers, known to
all the world now as Aucas.

Committing themselves and all their carefully laid plans to Him who had so unmistakably
brought them thus far, they waited for the Aucas.

Before four-thirty that afternoon the quiet
waters of the Curaray flowed over the bodies of the
five comrades, slain by the men they had come to
win for Christ, whose banner they had borne. The

world called it a nightmare of tragedy. The world did not recognize the truth of the second clause in Jim Elliot's credo: "He is no fool who gives what he cannot keep to gain what he cannot lose." ☆

———————

ELISABETH ELLIOT WAS BORN IN Brussels, Belgium, where her parents served as missionaries. After graduating from Wheaton College, she went to Ecuador as a missionary. In 1953, she married former classmate and fellow missionary, Jim Elliot. Their daughter, Valerie, was born in 1955. Ten months later, Jim was killed by the Auca Indians. Elisabeth continued her work as a missionary and later lived and worked among the Aucas. Elisabeth is the author of numerous books, including *These Strange Ashes, Through Gates of Splendor, Passion and Purity,* and *A Chance to Die: The Life and Legacy of Amy Carmichael.*

SHADOW OF THE ALMIGHTY
Paper, 256 pages
© 1958 by Elisabeth Elliot.
Introduction © 1989 by Elisabeth Elliot. All rights reserved.
Reprinted here by permission from Harper*SanFrancisco*, a
Division of HarperCollins Publishers.
ISBN: 006062213X

∽ CHRISTIAN LIVING ∽

31 Days of Praise
RUTH MYERS WITH WARREN MYERS

Christians who long to experience God in a fresh, deep way will treasure this powerful, personal praise guide.

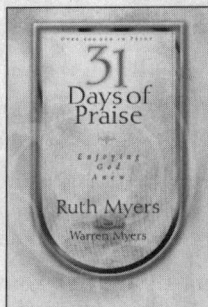

Day Three

I PRAISE YOU THAT the Lord Jesus lived His life sinlessly, in total accord with reality, with no falseness, no self-deception, no dark secrets, nothing to regret, nothing to be ashamed of...that He proclaimed the truth, the one utterly reliable foundation for our thinking and living. Thank You that He delighted to do Your will...that He withdrew for time alone in Your presence...that He was attentive to Your voice and sensitive to Your working...that

He lived in complete dependence on You, so that
You in Him spoke those gracious and life-giving
words and performed those mighty works.

Thank You that He demonstrated how I am to
live and serve, completely depending on Him as my
indwelling Lord, focusing on His life as He walked
on earth, and beholding His glory, "the glory of the
one and only" who came from You, full of grace
and truth. What a delight to know that as I focus on
Him, You transform me into His image by Your
Spirit within me....

Day Seven

I glorify You for the Bible—that wonderful,
written revelation of You and Your plan. As snow
and rain fall from the skies to meet our needs, so
You have condensed Your thoughts—which are
vastly higher than all human thoughts—into writ-
ten-down form. I'm so grateful that You cared
enough to communicate with us in this clear,
unchanging, always-accessible way, so that Your
thoughts are now available at all times to refresh
and nourish and teach me...and that You are still
a communicating God, speaking these words to
me as I am attentive to You, as I read and meditate
with a listening heart....

Thank You that in Your Word I can see Your
face and hear Your voice. I can discover Your will
and Your patterns for living and serving. I can
develop deeper faith and confidence. Thank You

that the Holy Spirit inspired Your Word and uses it to enlighten and guide me, and to change me more and more into Your image, from one degree of glory to another.

Day Ten

I choose to thank You for my weaknesses, my infirmities, my inadequacies (physical, mental, emotional, relational)...for the ways I fall short of what people view as ideal...for my feelings of helplessness and inferiority, and even my pain and distresses. What a comfort it is to know that You understand the feeling of my weaknesses!...and that in Your infinite wisdom You have allowed these in my life so that they may contribute to Your high purposes for me....

Thank You that many a time my weaknesses cut through my pride and help me walk humbly with You...and then, as You've promised, You give me more grace—You help and bless and strengthen me. Thank You for all the ways I'm inadequate, for they prod me to trust in You and not in myself...and I'm grateful that my adequacy comes from You, the all-sufficient God who is enough!

Thank You that I can trust You to remove or change any of my weaknesses and handicaps and shortcomings the moment they are no longer needed for Your glory, and for my good, and for the good of other people...and that in the meantime,

Your grace is sufficient for me, for Your strength is made perfect in my weakness.

Day Eleven

...How I thank You, Lord Jesus, that on the cross You bore my griefs and carried my sorrows, as well as my sins...that I can kneel at the cross and worship You as the One who took on Yourself all my pain and experienced it to the full. And how comforting to know that in the present, day by day, You feel with me any pain, confusion, inner bondage, or struggles that stem from my past. Thank You that all these seeming disadvantages are a backdrop for the special, unfolding plan You have in mind for me...and that if my past still handicaps me, You are able to lead me to the kind of help I need...

Day Fourteen

Father, I'm so glad that the Holy Spirit is within me, to strengthen me with power in my inner person...to make Christ real within me and flood my heart with His limitless love...to fill me with Your fullness...to enable me to know in personal experience the things You have so freely bestowed on me in Christ—my new identity, my incredible spiritual blessings.

I celebrate the fact that I have been crucified with Christ, and that now I am alive with His life...that through my new birth I died out of my old life, and that You resurrected me to a living relationship with You...and so I am dead to sin and alive to You! Thank You that these facts are true, whether or not they seem logical, whether or not I feel they're true...and that as I praise You for them, Your Spirit enables me more and more to live in the light of my new identity in You. Thank You that He is using Your Word to deliver me from the viewpoints and values of the world, the flesh, and the devil...and He is renewing my mind to see things from Your point of view, so that I can walk in newness of life....

Day Seventeen

Thank You that You have me in the place You want me just now...that even if I got here through wrong choices or indifference or even rebellion, yet You knew my mistakes and sins before I ever existed, and You worked them into Your plan to draw me to Yourself, to mold and bless me, and to bless others through me. Thank You that even if I'm here through the ill will or poor judgment of other people, all is well; for in Your sovereign wisdom You are at work to bring about good results from all those past decisions, those past events beyond my control—good results both for me and for others.

Thank You again that You meant for good the terrible things that happened to Joseph, who was sold into slavery, exiled to a distant country, and later sent to prison on false accusations...and that through all this You had him in the right place at the right time, for highly important reasons. I'm glad, Lord, that You are the same today—well able to work things out for us, to turn evil into good. I stand amazed at the complexity and mystery of Your wisdom. How safe it is for me to trust Your reasons for acting (or not acting) and Your methods of working!...

Day Eighteen

Father, I'm so delighted that You are both loving and sovereign, and that You cause all things to work together for good to those who love You, to those who are called according to Your purpose. So I thank You for each disturbing or humbling situation in my life, for each breaking or cleansing process You are allowing, for each problem or hindrance, for each thing that triggers in me anxiety or anger or pain. And I thank You in advance for each disappointment, each demanding duty, each pressure each interruption that may arise in the coming hours and days...

In spite of what I think or feel when I get my eyes off You, I choose not to resist my trials as intruders, but to welcome them as friends....

Day Twenty

Father, I thank You for the people in my life who seem to bring more pain than joy, for I believe You have let our paths cross for important reasons. Thank You for the good things You want to do in my life through the things that bother me (their irritating habits? their moodiness? their unloving ways? their demands? their insensitivity? their unrealistic expectations?). I'm grateful that You are with me to meet my needs when others—even those close to me—fail to do so. I'm so glad that You are also within me, working to make me more like Jesus—more patient, more gentle, more loving— through the very things I dislike....

Day Twenty-three

Thank You that You plan to use for good the struggles my loved ones face—including their disappointing choices, their unwise or even harmful ways of thinking and living, and their sidetracks from going Your way (as I see it—and, Lord, I know I could be wrong!).

I praise You in advance for the part these difficult things are going to play in Your good plan for us—in eventual deliverance and growth and fruitfulness. I'm grateful that in all these things the battle is not mine but Yours...and that the final chapter has not yet been written. How good it is that I can call on You to give me wisdom to know what to say or not say, what to do and not do...and that You live in me so that I can love with Your love, even when it's hard. Thank You that these trials force me to trust You more!...

Day Twenty-five

Dear Lord, how much I appreciate Your

viewpoint regarding human status and abilities, failures and weaknesses....

How glad I am that You don't expect perfect performance. "You are quick to mark every simple effort to please You, and just as quick to overlook imperfections when I meant to do Your will" (Tozer). You are full of mercy and compassion toward me. You know the way I'm put together; You know my limitations; You understand that I am dust. And I praise You that You are greater than any or all of my failures...that as my Potter, You are able to mold and remold me, as I submit to Your wisdom and skill...that as the Master Artist, You are able to take the dark threads of my life—my wounds, my scars, my blotches, the messes I make, and even my sins—and blend them into a beautiful design, to the praise of the glory of Your grace....

Day Twenty-nine

...Thank You that I can give myself up to be led by You...that I can go forth praising and at rest, letting You manage me and my day...that I can joyfully depend on You throughout the day, expecting You to guide, to enlighten, to reprove, to teach, to use, and to do in me and with me what You desire....

Day Thirty

...Thank You that You made Your light shine in my heart to give the light of the knowledge of Your glory in the face of Your Son...that You drew me to Yourself, and honored me, making me a member of Your royal family and a citizen of Your Kingdom...and that You have enlisted me in Your worldwide task force, to be Your witness. What a high privilege, that You have destined me to have a share not only in Your love but also in Your glorious purposes, both near and far...that You have gifted me for a unique part in Your global search for people who will repent and believe and learn to live for Your glory. I celebrate my high calling of knowing You and making You known! And I praise You for giving me Your Holy Spirit to fill and empower me, and for promising to be with me always....

Day Thirty-one

I exult before You because You are eternal and never-changing in Your truth, in Your attributes, and in Your attitude toward me and all Your loved ones. I'm so glad that Your persistent tenderness binds my heart to You forever...that You who began a good work in me will carry it to completion until the day of Christ Jesus. You are utterly faithful and will finish what You have set out to do. You will not abandon the work You have begun.... �֍

―――――――

RUTH MYERS AND HER LATE husband, Warren, served with

The Navigators in Singapore for many years, teaching men and women how to experience God and His Word. Together, they coauthored several books and Bible studies. Ruth lives in Colorado Springs, CO.

ADAPTED FROM 31 DAYS OF PRAISE

Hardcover, 160 pages

© 1994 by Warren and Ruth Myers

Used by permission of Multnomah Publishers Inc. All rights reserved.

ISBN: 1-57673-875-2

∾ CHRISTIAN LIVING ∾

The Pursuit of God

A. W. Tozer

During an all-night train trip, A.W. Tozer wrote The Pursuit of God *with such depth, clarity, and completeness that it remains an enduring favorite.*

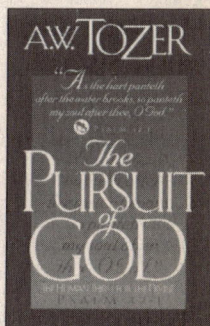

My soul followeth hard after thee:
thy right hand upholdeth me. (Psalm 63:8)

CHRISTIAN THEOLOGY TEACHES THE doctrine of prevenient grace, which, briefly stated, means that before a man can seek God, God must first have sought the man.

Before a sinful man can think a right thought of God, there must have been a work of enlightenment done within him. Imperfect it may be, but a true work nonetheless, and the secret cause of all desiring and seeking and praying which may follow.

We pursue God because, and only because, He has first put an urge within us that spurs us to the pursuit. "No man can come to me," said our Lord, "except the Father which hath sent me draw him," and it is by this *prevenient* drawing that God takes from us every vestige of credit for the act of coming. The impulse to pursue God originates with God, but the outworking of that impulse is our following hard after Him. All the time we are pursuing Him we are already in His hand: "Thy right hand upholdeth me."

In this divine "upholding" and human "following" there is no contradiction. All is of God, for as von Hügel teaches, *God is always previous.* In practice, however, (that is, where God's previous working meets man's present response) man must pursue God. On our part there must be positive reciprocation if this secret drawing of God is to eventuate in identifiable experience of the Divine. In the warm language of personal feeling, this is stated in Psalm 42:1–2: "As the hart panteth after the water brooks, so panteth my soul after thee, O God. My soul thirsteth for God, for the living God: when shall I come and appear before God?" This is deep calling unto deep, and the longing heart will understand it.

The doctrine of justification by faith—a biblical

truth, and a blessed relief from sterile legalism and unavailing self-effort—has in our time fallen into evil company and been interpreted by many in such a manner as actually to bar men from the knowledge of God. The whole transaction of religious conversion has been made mechanical and spiritless. Faith may now be exercised without a jar to the moral life and without embarrassment to the Adamic ego. Christ may be "received" without creating any special love for Him in the soul of the receiver. The man is "saved," but he is not hungry nor thirsty after God. In fact, he is specifically taught to be satisfied and is encouraged to be content with little.

The modern scientist has lost God amid the wonders of His world; we Christians are in real danger of losing God amid the wonders of His Word. We have almost forgotten that God is a person and, as such, can be cultivated as any person can. It is inherent in personality to be able to know other personalities, but full knowledge of one personality by another cannot be achieved in one encounter. It is only after long and loving mental intercourse that the full possibilities of both can be explored.

All social intercourse between human beings is a response of personality to personality, grading upward from the most casual brush between man and man to the fullest, most intimate communion of which the human soul is capable. Religion, so far as it is genuine, is in essence the response of created personalities to the creating personality, God. . . .

God is a person, and in the deep of His mighty nature He thinks, wills, enjoys, feels, loves, desires, and suffers as any other person may. In making Himself known to us He stays by the familiar pattern of personality. He communicates with us through the avenues of our minds, our wills and our emotions. The continuous and unembarrassed interchange of love and thought between God and the soul of the redeemed man is the throbbing heart of New Testament religion.

This intercourse between God and the soul is known to us in conscious personal awareness. It is personal: it does not stay below the threshold of consciousness and work there unknown to the soul (as, for instance, infant baptism is thought by some to do), but comes within the field of awareness where the man can know it as he knows any other fact of experience.

You and I are in little (our sins excepted) what God is in large. Being made in His image we have within us the capacity to know Him. In our sins we lack only the power. The moment the Spirit has quickened us to life in regeneration our whole being senses its kinship to God and leaps up in joyous recognition. That is the heavenly birth without which we cannot see the Kingdom of God. It is, however, not an end but an inception, for now begins the glorious pursuit, the heart's happy exploration of the infinite riches of the Godhead. That is where we begin, I say, but where we stop no man has yet discovered, for there is in the awful and mysterious depths of the Triune God neither limit nor end. . . .

To have found God and still to pursue Him is the soul's paradox of love, scorned indeed by the too-easily-satisfied religionist, but justified in happy experience by the children of the burning heart. St. Bernard stated this holy paradox in a musical quatrain that will be instantly understood by every worshiping soul:

> We taste Thee, O Thou Living Bread,
>   And long to feast upon Thee still:
> We drink of Thee, the Fountainhead
>   And thirst our souls from Thee to fill.

Come near to the holy men and women of the past and you will soon feel the heat of their desire after God. They mourned for Him, they prayed and wrestled and sought for Him day and night, in season and out, and when they had found Him the finding was all the sweeter for the long seeking. Moses used the fact that he knew God as an argument for knowing Him better. "Now therefore, I pray thee, if I have found grace in thy sight, shew me now thy way, that I may know thee, that I may find grace in thy sight" (Exodus 33:13); and from there he rose to make the daring request, "I beseech thee, shew me thy glory" (33:18). God was frankly pleased by this display of ardor, and the next day called

Moses into the mount, and there in solemn procession made all His glory pass before him. . . .

Hymnody is sweet with the longing after God, the God whom, while the singer seeks, he knows he has already found. "His track I see and I'll pursue," sang our fathers only a short generation ago, but that song is heard no more in the great congregation. How tragic that we in this dark day have had our seeking done for us by our teachers. Everything is made to center upon the initial act of "accepting" Christ (a term, incidentally, which is not found in the Bible) and we are not expected thereafter to crave any further revelation of God to our souls. We have been snared in the coils of a spurious logic which insists that if we have found Him, we need no more seek Him. This is set before us as the last word in orthodoxy, and it is taken for granted that no Bible-taught Christian ever believed otherwise. Thus the whole testimony of the worshiping, seeking, singing church on that subject is crisply set aside. The experiential heart-theology of a grand army of fragrant saints is rejected in favor of a smug interpretation of Scripture which would certainly have sounded strange to an Augustine, a Rutherford or a Brainerd.

In the midst of this great chill there are some, I rejoice to acknowledge, who will not be content with shallow logic. They will admit the force of the argument, and then turn away with tears to hunt some lonely place and pray, "O God, show me Thy glory." They want to taste, to touch with their hearts, to see with their inner eyes the wonder that is God.

I want deliberately to encourage this mighty longing after God. The lack of it has brought us to our present low estate. The stiff and wooden quality about our religious lives is a result of our lack of holy desire. Complacency is a deadly foe of all spiritual growth. Acute desire must be present or there will be no manifestation of Christ to His people. He waits to be wanted. Too bad that with many of us He waits so long, so very long, in vain.

Every age has its own characteristics. Right now we are in an age of religious complexity. The simplicity which is in Christ is rarely found among us. In its stead are programs, methods, organizations and a world of nervous activities which occupy time and attention but can never satisfy the longing of the heart. The shallowness of our inner experience, the hollowness of our worship, and that servile imitation of the world which marks our promotional methods all testify that we, in this day, know God only imperfectly, and the peace of God scarcely at all.

If we would find God amid all the religious externals, we must first determine to find Him, and then proceed in the way of simplicity. Now, as always, God discovers Himself to "babes" and hides Himself in thick darkness from the wise and the prudent. We must simplify our approach to Him.

We must strip down to essentials (and they will be found to be blessedly few). We must put away all effort to impress, and come with the guileless candor of childhood. If we do this, without doubt God will quickly respond.

When religion has said its last word, there is little that we need other than God Himself. The evil habit of seeking *God-and* effectively prevents us from finding God in full revelation. In the *and* lies our great woe. If we omit the *and* we shall soon find God, and in Him we shall find that for which we have all our lives been secretly longing.

We need not fear that in seeking God only we may narrow our lives or restrict the motions of our expanding hearts. The opposite is true. We can well afford to make God our All, to concentrate, to sacrifice the many for the One. . . .

The man who has God for his treasure has all things in One. Many ordinary treasures may be denied him, or if he is allowed to have them, the enjoyment of them will be so tempered that they will never be necessary to his happiness. Or if he must see them go, one after one, he will scarcely feel a sense of loss, for having the Source of all things he has in One all satisfaction, all pleasure, all delight. Whatever he may lose he has actually lost nothing, for he now has it all in One, and he has it purely, legitimately and forever.

God, I have tasted Thy goodness, and it has both satisfied me and made me thirsty for more. I am painfully conscious of my

*need of further grace. I am ashamed of my lack of desire. O God,
the Triune God, I want to want Thee; I long to be filled with longing; I thirst to be made more thirsty still. Show me Thy glory, I
pray Thee, that so I may know Thee indeed. Begin in mercy a new
work of love within me. Say to my soul, "Rise up, my love, my fair
one, and come away." Then give me grace to rise and follow Thee
up from this misty lowland where I have wandered so long.*

In Jesus' name. Amen. ☀

AIDEN WILSON TOZER WAS BORN April 21, 1897, in La Jose
(now Newburg), a tiny farming community in western
Pennsylvania. He came to Christ at age 17. In 1919, Tozer
began 44 years of ministry with The Christian and Missionary
Alliance. For 31 of those years, he gained prominence as pastor of Southside Alliance Church in Chicago and as the editor
of *Alliance Life* magazine for which he wrote many provocative
editorials. Tozer died in 1963. His greatest legacy to the
Christian world has been his more than 40 books, including
The Pursuit of God.

THE PURSUIT OF GOD
Paper, 122 pages
© 1982, 1993 by Christian Publications Inc.
All rights reserved.
ISBN: 0875093663

⮫ POETRY ⮬

Mountain Breezes: The Collected Poems of Amy Carmichael

AMY CARMICHAEL

Through this remarkable collection of 568 of Amy Carmichael's best-loved poems, she speaks to the deepest places in each of us.

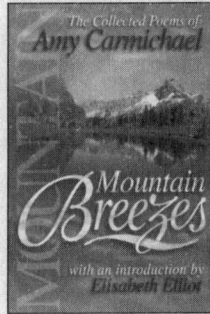

No Scar?

> Hast thou no scar?
> No hidden scar on foot, or side, or hand?
> I hear thee sung as mighty in the land;
> I hear them hail thy bright, ascendant star.
> Hast *thou* no scar?

Hast thou no wound?
Yet I was wounded by the archers; spent,
Leaned Me against a tree to die; and rent
By ravening beasts that compassed Me, I swooned.
Hast thou no wound?

No wound? No scar?
Yet, as the Master shall the servant be,
And pierced are the feet that follow Me.
But thine are whole; can he have followed far
Who has nor wound nor scar?

Royal Scars

We follow a scarred Captain;
    Should we not have scars?
Under His faultless orders
    We follow to the wars.
Lest we forget, Lord, when we meet,
    Show us Thy hands and feet.

O wounded One, most Royal,
    Who wert set at nought,
No trumpets were, no banners
    On field our Captain fought.
When we forget and seek for stars,
Show us Thy wounds, Thy scars.

Two Swords

Thy sword was bathed in heaven;
And that great sword
Bathed in clear glory, Lord,
Has conquered me—
And conquering, set me free.

Oh, bathe my sword in heaven,
Lest creeping rust
Or stain of earthly dust,
Dim the bright blade
Pledged to my Lord's crusade.

Thy sword, bathed in high heaven,
Purged ancient wrongs;
To Thee my sword belongs
For that same fight.
Bathe it, O Lord, in light.

Divine Paradox

But all through life I see a cross
Where sons of God yield up their breath:
There is no gain except by loss,
There is no life except by death;
And no full vision but by faith
Nor glory but by bearing shame,
Nor justice but by taking blame.
And that Eternal Passion saith:
"Be emptied of glory and right and name."

The Shell

Upon the sandy shore an empty shell,
    Beyond the shell infinity of sea;
O Savior, I am like that empty shell,
    Thou art the Sea to me.

A sweeping wave rides up the shore, and lo,
    Each dim recess the coiled shell within
Is searched, is filled, is filled to overflow
    By water crystalline.

Not to the shell is any glory then:
    All glory give we to the glorious sea.
And not to me is any glory when
    Thou overflowest me.

Sweep over me, Thy shell, as low I lie;
    I yield me to the purpose of Thy will;
Sweep up, O conquering waves, and purify,
    And with Thy fullness fill.

Forget the Shell

An empty shell lay by the sea;
    The waves rolled up, and all forgot
To think of that which mattered not;
    They only saw the sea.

So be it, Lord; let this Thy shell
    Be lost in glory of the sea;
And as the waves sweep over me,
    Let all forget the shell.

O Wave of God

O Wave of God, arise and overflow
High watermark on this our stretch of shore.
Great Wave of God, deal with us till we know
Something beyond all we have known before—
Far, far beyond all we have known before.

O Following Wave, from utmost Deeps arise;
We yield to Thy majestic urgency;
Forbid we ever or in anywise
Refuse to yield our all, lose all in Thee;
Sweep on, O Wave, we yield ourselves to Thee.

How Can I Not Love Much?

O King of Love, Thy royal ways
    With thy poor vassal pass my thought.
What word can fitly frame Thy praise?
Thy love illuminates my days—
    Love to a thing of nought.

O Lord of Love, how privily
    Thou comest; and Thy finger's touch
On hidden string, known but to Thee,
Attunes to sweetness all in me.
    Loved so, how not love much?

But what is much? Rock-pool to sea,
    Faint taper to a furnace glow?
O Love, who art Infinity,
Whose secret source no man may see,
    Flow through me, overflow.

All My Fountains

(*Psalm 87:7*)

"All my fountains are in Thee,"
Word of mountain mystery:
    Higher than earth's flowers grow,
    Far above the highest snow,
    Lies the watershed
    Whence my stream is fed.

Living fountain, now I pray:
Let no boulder block the way;
    If such hindering thing there be
    Lurking deep in pool, in me,
    Mighty floods sweep down
    And uproot that stone.

They that sing and they that dance
Bring me word of jubilance:
    Never need my stream run low,
    Waters never cease to flow
    From the hills afar,
    Where my fountains are.

Fulfill Me Now with Love

Father of spirits, this my earnest plea
I bring again and yet again to Thee:
Fulfill me now with love, that I may know
A daily inflow, daily overflow.

For love—for love my Lord was crucified;
With cords of love He bound me to His side.
Pour through me now; I yield myself to Thee,
O Love that led my Lord to Calvary.

Pour Love Through Me

Love of God, eternal Love,
    Sweep my barriers down!
Fountain of eternal love,
    Let Thy power be known;
Fill me, flood me, overflow me;
Love of God, eternal Love,
    Sweep my barriers down!

Love of God, eternal Love,
    Pour Thy love through me!
Nothing less than Calvary love
    Do I ask of Thee;
Fill me, flood me, overflow me;
Love of God, eternal Love,
    Pour Thy love through me!

Love's Overflow

Spirit of Wind, Spirit of Fire,
    Fulfill in me Thy great desire;
Enter and purge each hidden cell—
    That Christ in me may dwell.

That I be rooted fast in love,
    And in that love may live and move,
O Love Eternal, let me know
    Love's mighty overflow.

Tune Thou My Harp

Tune Thou my harp;
There is not, Lord, could never be,
The skill in me.

Tune Thou my harp,
That it may play Thy melody,
Thy harmony.

Tune Thou my harp;
O Spirit, breathe Thy thought through me,
As pleaseth Thee.

Lord of Music

Let me sing your song, ye waters;
    Bid your falls their voices lend—
Let your thousand springing daughters
    Each to me be kindly friend.
Swept up in their nobler music,
    Let my poor earth tunes have end.

What am I but dust and ashes?
    Ye alone are clear and pure;
Passing I, as passing flashes
    Light upon you; ye endure.

Take my falt'ring chords and lose them
　　In your glorious overture.

Oh, ye fail me; turn I rather,
　　Lord of music, unto Thee.
In the Kingdom of Thy Father,
　　Tender all the judgments be.
Take my human alleluias;
　　Perfect Thou the harmony.

A Joy to Thee

Let me see Thy face, Lord Jesus,
　　Caring not for aught beside;
Let me hear Thy voice, Lord Jesus,
　　Till my soul is satisfied.

Let me walk with Thee, Lord Jesus;
　　Let me walk in step with Thee.
Let me talk with Thee, Lord Jesus;
　　Let Thy words be clear to me.

Heavenly music, strength and sweetness,
　　Joy of joys art Thou to me;
O Beloved, my Lord Jesus,
　　Let me be a joy to Thee.

To See and Know Him

My heart said unto Thee:
My face would seek Thy face;
O Lord, grant me this grace:
Shine down on me.

176

Myself would cloud my skies.
Let self be crucified;
Let love be fortified;
Anoint mine eyes.

Thee would I see and know;
All else would I forget.
Let Thy fair beauty set
My life aglow.

Following

I follow where Thou leadest; what are bruises?
There are cool leaves of healing on Thy tree;
Lead Thou me on. Thy heavenly wisdom chooses
        In love for me.

Thy lover then, like happy homing swallow
That crosses hill and plain and lonely sea,
All unafraid, so I will fearless follow,
        For love of Thee.

Our Undefeated Lord

O undefeated Lord,
    Where Thou art, there are we;
Out on the battlefield
    our sword unsheathed would be.
We fall but to arise,
    For Thou dost never fall—
And in Thy steadfast eyes
    We read again our call.

We read it and rejoice;
    Oh, perish every fear;
Thy pard'ning, heart'ning voice
    Is sounding in our ear.
Thrice blessed be Thy word
    To us—to me—to me!
O undefeated Lord,
    Lead on; we follow Thee.

Make Me Thy Fuel

From prayer that asks that I may be
Sheltered from winds that beat on Thee,
From fearing when I should aspire,
From faltering when I should climb higher,
From silken self, O Captain, free
Thy soldier who would follow Thee.

From subtle love of softening things,
From easy choices, weakenings,
(Not thus are spirits fortified,
Not this way went the Crucified)
From all that dims Thy Calvary,
O Lamb of God, deliver me.

Give me the love that leads the way,
The faith that nothing can dismay,
The hope no disappointments tire,
The passion that will burn like fire;
Let me not sink to be a clod:
Make me Thy fuel, Flame of God.

———————

"NOTHING IS IMPORTANT BUT THAT which is eternal." This was the foundation for Amy Carmichael's life and ministry. Amy was an instrument chosen by God who spent most of her life in India where she founded the Dohnavur Fellowship, a ministry dedicated to rescuing children from temple prostitution and raising them for Christ. Her books and poetry have inspired millions, as has her uncompromising determination to be consumed on the altar of sacrificial love. Her top-selling books include *If, Edges of His Ways, Mimosa, Whispers of His Power,* and more.

MOUNTAIN BREEZES
Hardcover, 472 pages
Paper, 472 pages
© 1999 The Dohnavur Fellowship
CLC Publications
ISBNs: 0-87508-790-6, hardcover; -789-2, paper

∽ RELIGIOUS FICTION ∽
The Pilgrim's Progress
JOHN BUNYAN
EDITED AND MODERNIZED BY HAL M. HELMS

Deemed the greatest
allegory ever written,
The Pilgrim's Progress
is the classic story of
an awakened soul on
its perilous journey to
the Celestial City.

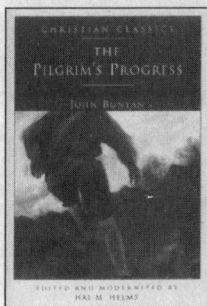

Chapter I

AS I WALKED THROUGH the wilderness of this world, I lighted on a certain place where there was a Den, and I lay down there to sleep. As I slept, I dreamed a dream.

Behold, I saw a man clothed with rags, standing with his face looking away from his own house, a Book in his hand, and a great burden on his back. As I looked, he opened the Book, and read in it, and as he read, he wept and trembled. Not being able to contain himself any longer, he began to weep, saying, "What shall I do?"

In this same condition, he turned and went back to his home, trying as best he could to keep his wife and children from seeing his distress. He could not be silent long, however, because his troubles seemed to increase. At length, he began to share with his wife and children what was in his mind. "Oh, my dear wife, and you, the children I love, I am undone by this burden that lies too heavy on my back. And more than this, I am told that our city is going to be burned with fire from heaven, and that both you and myself will come to ruin unless some way can be found for us to escape. I haven't found the way yet."

His family was amazed and did not believe what he said was true. They thought that some madness had seized him. Hoping that sleep would settle his mind, they hurried him off to bed. But the night was as troublesome to him as the day, and instead of sleeping, he spent the night in sighs and tears.

When the morning came, his family wanted to know how he was. "Worse and worse," he said. He began talking to them again about his burden and his fears, but they would hear none of it. Their hearts were hardening, and they hoped by such things as harsh words they could jolt this foolishness out of him. Sometimes they would make fun of him, sometimes they would chide him, sometimes neglect him. So he began to spend more time in his own room, where he would pray for them and would grieve over his own misery. At times he would walk out in the countryside; sometimes he would read, sometimes pray. Days passed.

Then I saw him walking in the fields, reading his Book, as he liked to do, and as he read, he burst out as he had done at the beginning, crying, "What shall I do to be saved?"

He looked this way and that, as if he wanted to run; yet he stood still, because (as I understood) he could not tell which way to go. Then I saw a man named Evangelist, who came to him and asked, "Why are you crying?"

The man answered, "Sir, I understand by the Book in my hand that I am condemned to die, and after that to come to judgment. I find that I am not willing to die and am not ready to come to judgment."

Evangelist said, "Why are you not willing to die, since this life contains so many evils?"

The man answered, "Because I fear that this burden on my back will sink me lower than the grave and I will fall into the depths of hell. And, sir, if I am not fit to go to prison, I am not fit to go to judgment, and from thence to be executed; and the thought of these things make me cry."

Then said Evangelist, "If this is your condition, why do you stand still?"

"Because I do not know where to go," he answered.

Then Evangelist gave him a parchment roll on which were written the words, "Flee from the wrath to come." The man therefore read it and, looking at Evangelist very carefully, asked, "Which way must I flee?" Evangelist pointed with his finger over a very wide space and asked, "Do you see that narrow gate yonder?"

The man said, "No."

"Do you see yonder shining light?" Evangelist asked.

"I *think* I do, " the man replied.

Evangelist continued, "Keep that light in your eye and go directly to it. In this way you will see the gate. When you knock at the gate, you will be told what to do."

So I saw in my dream that the man began to run. Now, he had not run far from his own door when his wife and children, perceiving that he was leaving, began to call to him to return. But the man put his fingers in his ears, and ran on, crying, "Life! life! eternal life!"

So he looked not behind him, but ran toward the middle of the plain.

Chapter 2

The neighbors also came out to see the man

run, and as he ran, some mocked, others threatened and some cried after him to return.

Among those who came out, two were resolved to bring him back by force if necessary. The name of one was Obstinate, and the name of the other, Pliable.

By this time, the man had gotten a good distance ahead of them. As they pursued him, however, they shortly overtook him, and he turned to them asking, "Neighbors, why are you coming after me?"

"To persuade you to come back with us," they answered.

The man replied, "That can by no means be. You dwell in the City of Destruction, the place where I, also, was born. I see now that it is indeed the City of Destruction, and dying there, sooner of later, you will sink lower than the grave into a place that burns with fire and brimstone. So, good neighbors, be content and go along with me."

"What!" said Obstinate, "and leave our friends and comforts behind us?"

"Yes," said Christian (for that was his name), "because all you forsake is not worthy to be compared with a little of what I am seeking to enjoy. If you would go along with me and hold it, you shall fare as I myself. For where I am going there is enough and to spare. Come then, and prove my words."

"What are the things you seek, since you leave

all the world behind?" asked Obstinate.

"I seek, " said Christian, "an inheritance incorruptible, undefiled, and that fades not away, one that is laid up in heaven and is safe there, to be bestowed at the time appointed on those who diligently seek it. Read it so, if you will, in my Book."

"Tush!" said Obstinate. "Away with your book; will you go back with us or not?"

"No, not I," said the other, "because I have put my hand to the plow."

Obstinate turned to Pliable and said, "Come then, neighbor Pliable. Let us turn back and go home without him. There is a company of these crazy-headed fools who are wiser in their own eyes than seven men who can reason with them."

Pliable said, "Don't revile. If what the good Christian says is true, the things he looks for are better than ours. My heart inclines to go with my neighbor."

"What? more fools still?" snorted Obstinate. "Listen to me and go back. Who knows where such a muddle-headed fellow as this will lead you? Go back, go back and be wise!"

Christian then exclaimed, "Nay! Come with me, Pliable! There are such things to be had which I spoke of, and many more glorious ones besides. If you can't believe me, here, read it in this Book. The truth of what is written in it is all confirmed by the Blood of Him who made it."

"Well, neighbor Obstinate," said Pliable, "I

begin to come to a decision. I am going along with this good man. But, my good companion, do you know the way to this desired place?"

"I am directed by a man whose name is Evangelist," replied Christian, "to speed to a little narrow gate that lies before us, where we will receive instructions about the Way."

"Come then, good neighbor," answered Pliable, "let us be going."

So they both went along together.

"And I will go back to my place," shouted Obstinate over his shoulder. "I will be no companion of such misled, fanatical fellows."

I saw in my dream that when Obstinate left, Christian and Pliable went walking over the plain, talking together as they went.

"Come, neighbor Pliable, how are you doing? I am glad you were persuaded to go along with me. Had even Obstinate himself but felt what I have felt of the powers and terrors of what is yet unseen, he would not so lightly have turned his back on us!"

Pliable replied, "My good neighbor, since there are only the two of us here, tell me now further about the wonderful things where we are going."

"I can better conceive them in my mind than I can put them into words," answered his companion. "But, since you desire to know, I will read of them in my Book."

"And do you think that the words of your Book are certainly true?" asked Pliable.

"Yes, verily, " Christian avowed. "This Book was made by Him who cannot lie."

"Well said! What wonderful things are they?"

"There is an endless kingdom to be inhabited, and everlasting life to be given us, that we may inhabit that kingdom forever."

"Well said! and what else?"

"There are crowns of glory to be given us, and garments that will make us shine like the sun in the heavens."

"This is very pleasant," continued Pliable. "And what else?"

"There shall be no more crying, nor sorrow, for He who is the Owner of the place will wipe away all tears from our eyes."

"And what company shall we have there?" asked Pliable.

"There we shall be with seraphim and cherubim," answered Christian, "creatures that shall dazzle your eyes to look on them. There also you will meet with thousands and ten thousands who have gone before us to that place. None of them are hurtful, but all are loving and holy; everyone is walking in the sight of God, standing in His presence forever. In a word, we shall see the elders with their golden crowns; there we shall see the holy virgins with their golden harps; there we shall see men who were cut in pieces by the world, burnt in flames, eaten by beasts, drowned in the seas – all for the love they bear to the Lord of that place. They will all be well and clothed with immortality as with a garment."

"Hearing this is enough to ravish one's heart!" exclaimed Pliable. "But are these things to be enjoyed? How shall we get to be sharers of them?"

"The Lord, the Governor of that country, has recorded all that in this Book," Christian went on. "The substance of it is this: if we are truly willing to have it, He will bestow it upon us freely."

"Well, my good companion, I am glad to hear of these things. Come on, let's increase our pace!"

Christian replied sadly, "I cannot go so fast as I would because of this burden on my back."

I saw in my dream that just as they ended this talk, they came to a very miry swamp in the middle of the plain. Not noticing it, they both fell suddenly into it. It is called the Slough of Despond. Here they wallowed for a time, and were grievously covered with dirt and mud. Christian, because of the burden on his back, began to sink in the mire.

Then Pliable called out, "Ah! neighbor Christian, where are you now?"

John Bunyan was born in England in 1628. As a youth, he overheard two Christians conversing about the joy of new birth and the work of God in men's hearts. It awakened him to his need of salvation through Jesus Christ. After his conversion, he became a remarkably effective preacher who was imprisoned by the governing authorities for his bold witness for Christ. *The Pilgrim's Progress* has captivated a vast readership rivaled only by that of the Bible and continues to provide inspiration and spiritual guidance for generations of readers.

THE PILGRIM'S PROGRESS
Paper, 268 pages
© 1982 by the Community of Jesus Inc.
Paraclete Press
ISBN: 0-941478-02-5

∽ INSPIRATIONAL ∽

My Utmost for His Highest
Oswald Chambers

For generations, Oswald Chambers' masterwork has been a best-seller. It strikes a chord with readers seeking real depth in a devotional. Several editions are available.

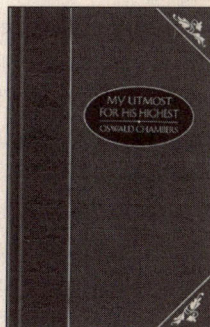

July 5
DON'T CALCULATE WITHOUT GOD

"Commit thy way unto the Lord; trust also in Him; and He shall bring it to pass."
Psalm 37:5

Don't calculate without God.

God seems to have a delightful way of upsetting the things we have calculated on without taking Him into account. We get into circumstances which were not chosen by God, and suddenly we find we have been calculating without God; He has not entered in as a living factor. The one thing that keeps us from the possibility of worrying is bringing God in as the greatest factor in all our calculations.

In our religion it is customary to put God first, but we are apt to think it is an impertinence to put Him first in the practical issues of our lives. If we imagine we have to put on our Sunday moods before we come near to God, we will never come near Him. We must come as we are.

Don't calculate with the evil in view.

Does God really mean us to take no account of the evil? "Love. . .taketh no account of the evil." Love is not ignorant of the existence of the evil, but it does not take it in as a calculating factor. Apart from God, we do reckon with evil; we calculate with it in view and work all our reasonings from that standpoint.

Don't calculate with the rainy day in view.

You cannot lay up for a rainy day if you are trusting Jesus Christ. Jesus said—"Let not your heart be troubled." God will not keep your heart from being troubled. It is a command—"Let not ..." Haul yourself up a hundred and one times a day in order to do it, until you get into the habit of putting God first and calculating with Him in view.

July 6
VISION AND REALITY

"And the parched ground shall become a pool."
Isaiah 35:7

We always have visions, before a thing is made real. When we realize that although the vision is real, it is not real in us, then is the time that Satan comes in with his temptations, and we are apt to say it is no use to go on. Instead of the vision becoming real, there has come the valley of humiliation.

Life is not as idle ore,
But iron dug from central gloom,
And batter'd by the shocks of doom
To shape and use.

God gives us the vision, then He takes us down to the valley to batter us into the shape of the vision, and it is in the valley that so many of us faint and give way. Every vision will be made real if we will have patience. Think of the enormous leisure of God! He is never in a hurry. We are always in such a frantic hurry. In the light of the glory of the vision we go forth to do things, but the vision is not real in us yet; and God has to take us into the valley, and put us through fires and floods to batter us into shape, until we get to the place where He can trust us with the veritable reality. Ever since we had the vision God has been at work, getting us into the shape of the ideal, and over and over again we escape from His hand and try to batter ourselves into our own shape.

The vision is not a castle in the air, but a vision of what God wants you to be. Let Him put you on His wheel and whirl you as He likes, and as sure as God is God and you are you, you will turn out exactly in accordance with the vision. Don't lose heart in the process. If you have ever had the vision of God, you may try as you like to be satisfied on a lower level, but God will never let you.

July 7
ALL NOBLE THINGS ARE DIFFICULT

"Enter ye in at the strait gate. . .because strait is
the gate, and narrow is the way. . . ."
Matthew 7:13–14

If we are going to live as disciples of Jesus, we have to remember that all noble things are difficult. The Christian life is gloriously difficult, but the difficulty of it does not make us faint and cave in, it rouses us up to overcome. Do we so appreciate the marvelous salvation of Jesus Christ that we are our utmost for His highest?

God saves men by His sovereign grace

through the Atonement of Jesus. He works in us to will and to do of His good pleasure; but we have to work out that salvation in practical living. If once we start on the basis of His Redemption to do what He commands, we find that we can do it. If we fail, it is because we have not practiced. The crisis will reveal whether we have been practicing or not. If we obey the Spirit of God and practice in our physical life what God has put in us by His Spirit, then when the crisis comes, we shall find that our own nature as well as the grace of God will stand by us.

Thank God He does give us difficult things to do! His salvation is a glad thing, but it is also a heroic, holy thing. It tests us for all we are worth. Jesus is bringing many "sons" unto glory, and God will not shield us from the requirements of a son. God's grace turns out men and women with a strong family likeness to Jesus Christ, not milksops. It takes a tremendous amount of discipline to live the noble life of a disciple of Jesus in actual things. It is always necessary to make an effort to be noble.

July 8
THE WILL TO LOYALTY

"Choose you this day whom ye will serve."
Joshua 24:15

Will is the whole man active. I cannot give up my will, I must exercise it. I must will to obey, and I must will to receive God's Spirit. When God gives a vision of truth it is never a question of what He will do, but of what we will do. The Lord has been putting before us all some big propositions, and the best thing to do is to remember what you did when you were touched by God before—the time when you were saved, or first saw Jesus, or realized some truth. It was easy then to yield allegiance to God; recall those moments now as the Spirit of God brings before you some new proposition.

"Choose you this day whom ye will serve." It is a deliberate calculation, not something into which you drift easily; and everything else is in abeyance until you decide. The proposition is between you and God; do not confer with flesh and blood about it. With every new proposition other people get more and more "out of it" that is where the strain comes. God allows the opinion of His saints to matter to you, and yet you are brought more and more out of the certainty that others understand the step you are taking. You have no business to find out where God is leading, the only thing God will explain to you is Himself.

Profess to Him—"I will be loyal." Immediately you choose to be loyal to Jesus Christ, you are a witness against yourself. Don't consult other Christians but profess before Him—I will serve Thee. Will to be loyal—and give other people credit for being loyal too.

July 9

THE GREAT PROBING

"Ye cannot serve the Lord."
Joshua 24:19

Have you the slightest reliance on anything other than God? Is there a remnant of reliance left on any natural virtue, any set of circumstances? Are you relying on yourself in any particular in this new proposition which God has put before you? That is what the probing means. It is quite true to say—"I cannot live a holy life," but you can decide to let Jesus Christ make you holy. "Ye cannot serve the Lord God"; but you can put yourself in the place where God's almighty power will come through you. Are you sufficiently right with God to expect Him to manifest His wonderful life in you?

"Nay, but we will serve the Lord." It is not an impulse, but a deliberate commitment. You say—But God can never have called me to this, I am too unworthy, it can't mean me. It does mean you, and the weaker and feebler you are, the better. The one who has something to trust in is the last one to come anywhere near saying—"I will serve the Lord."

We say—"If I really could believe!" The point is—If I really will believe. No wonder Jesus Christ lays such emphasis on the sin of unbelief. "And He did not many mighty works there because of their unbelief." If we really believed that God meant what

He said—what should we be like! Dare I really let
God be to me all that He says He will be?

July 10
THE SPIRITUAL SLUGGARD

"Let us consider one another to
provoke unto love and to good works:
not forsaking the assembling of ourselves together."
Hebrews 10:24–25

We are all capable of being spiritual sluggards; we do not want to mix with the rough and
tumble of life as it is, our one object is to secure
retirement. The note struck in Hebrews 10 is that
of provoking one another and of keeping together—
both of which require initiative, the initiative of
Christ realization, not of self-realization. To live a
remote, retired, secluded life is the antipodes of
spirituality as Jesus Christ taught it.

The test of our spirituality comes when we
come up against injustice and meanness and ingratitude and turmoil, all of which have the tendency to
make us spiritual sluggards. We want to use prayer
and Bible reading for the purpose of retirement.
We utilize God for the sake of getting peace and joy,
that is, we do not want to realize Jesus Christ, but
only our enjoyment of Him. This is the first step in
the wrong direction. All these things are effects and
we try to make them causes.

"I think it meet," said Peter, ". . .to stir you up by putting you in remembrance." It is a most disturbing thing to be smitten in the ribs by some provoker of God, by someone who is full of spiritual activity. Active work and spiritual activity are not the same thing. Active work may be the counterfeit of spiritual activity. The danger of spiritual sluggishness is that we do not wish to be stirred up, all we want to hear about is spiritual retirement. Jesus Christ never encourages the idea of retirement— "Go tell My brethren. . . ." ☀

OSWALD CHAMBERS (1874-1917), THE SON of a Scottish Baptist pastor, was converted under the ministry of Charles Spurgeon. Following formal theological training in Scotland, he traveled throughout the United Kingdom, the Far East, and the United States, lecturing on the Scriptures. In 1911, he founded the Bible Training Center in Clapham, London. After his death, his wife, a stenographer, compiled his books from lectures and published them.

My Utmost for His Highest
Hardcover, 288 pages
© 1963 by Oswald Chambers Publications Association Ltd.
Barbour Publishing Inc.
ISBN: 1-57748-914-4

∾ CHRISTIAN LIVING ∾
The Grace Awakening
CHARLES R. SWINDOLL

This classic has awakened readers to the untapped wonders of grace that can make the difference between ho-hum religion and an intimate relationship with God.

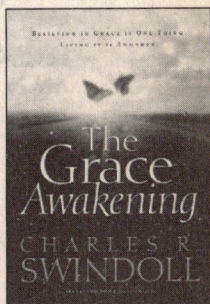

THERE ARE KILLERS ON the loose today. The problem is that you can't tell by looking. They don't wear little buttons that give away their identity, nor do they carry signs warning everybody to stay away. On the contrary, a lot of them carry Bibles and appear to be clean-living, nice-looking, law-abiding citizens. Most of them spend a lot of time in churches, some in places of religious leadership. Many are so respected in the community, their neighbors would never guess they are living next door to killers.

They kill freedom, spontaneity, and creativity; they kill joy as well as productivity. They kill with their words and their pens and their looks. They kill with their attitudes far more often than with their behavior. There is hardly a church or Christian organization or Christian school or missionary group or media ministry where such danger does not lurk. The amazing thing is that they get away with it, day in and day out, without being confronted or exposed. Strangely, the same ministries that would not tolerate heresy for ten minutes will step aside and allow these killers all the space they need to maneuver and manipulate others in the most insidious manner imaginable. Their intolerance is tolerated. Their judgmental spirits remain unjudged. Their bullying tactics continue unchecked. And their narrow-mindedness is either explained away or quickly defended.

This day—this very moment—millions who should be free, productive individuals are living in shame, fear, and intimidation. The tragedy is they think it is the way they should be. They have never known the truth that could set them free. They are victimized, existing as if they are living on death row instead of enjoying the beauty and fresh air of the abundant life Christ modeled and made possible for all of His followers to claim.

Unfortunately, most don't have a clue about what they are missing.

That whole package, in a word, is *grace*. That's what is being assaulted so continually, so violently. Those who aren't comfortable denying it have decided to debate it. But it is a classic no-win debate that trivializes the issue and leaves the masses who watch the fight from the stands confused, polarized, or, worst of all, bored. Grace was meant to be received and lived out to the fullest, not dissected and analyzed by those who would rather argue than eat. Enough of this! Grace must be awakened and released, not denied . . . enjoyed and freely given, not debated.

Grace received but unexpressed is dead grace. To spend one's time debating how grace is received or how much commitment is necessary for salvation, without getting into what it means to live by grace and enjoy the magnificent freedom it provides, quickly leads to a counterproductive argument. It becomes little more than another tedious trivial pursuit where the majority of God's people spend days looking back and asking, "How did we receive it?" instead of looking ahead and announcing, "Grace is ours . . . Let's live it!" Deny it or debate it, and we kill it. My plea is that we claim it and allow it to set us free. When we do, grace will become what it was meant to be—*really* amazing! When that happens, our whole countenance changes.

"No" Faces . . . "Yes" Faces

Dr. Karl Menninger, in a book entitled *The Vital Balance,* at one point discusses the negativistic personality. That's the type of person who says no to just about everything. Calling these sad folks "troubled patients," Menninger (no doubt with tongue in cheek) mentions several of the things that characterize their lives: They have never made an unsound loan, voted for a liberal cause, or sponsored any extravagances. Why? He suggests it is because they cannot permit themselves the pleasure of giving. He describes them in vivid terms: "rigid, chronically unhappy individuals, bitter, insecure, and often suicidal."[1]

I would add one further description—they have never given themselves permission to be free. Still imprisoned behind the bars of petty concerns and critical suspicions, they have learned to exist in a bondage that has hindered their ability to see beyond life's demands. Lacking grace, they have reduced life to the rules and regulations essential for survival. Their God is too small, their world is too rigid, and therefore their faces shout "No!"

Candidly, I know of nothing that has the power to change us from within like the freedom that comes through grace. It's so amazing it will change not only our hearts but also our faces. And goodness knows, some of us are overdue for a face change!

---

1. Dr. Karl Menninger, M. D., with Martin Mayman, Ph.D., and Paul Pruyser, Ph.D., *The Vital Balance* (New York: Viking Press, 1963), 204-205.

During his days as president, Thomas
Jefferson and a group of companions were traveling across the country on horseback. They came to
a river that had left its banks because of a recent
downpour. The swollen river had washed the
bridge away. Each rider was forced to ford the river
on horseback, fighting for his life against the rapid
currents. Each rider was threatened with the very
real possibility of death, which caused a traveler
who was not part of their group to step aside and
watch. After several had plunged in and made it to
the other side, the stranger asked President
Jefferson if he would carry him across the river.
The president agreed without hesitation. The man
climbed on, and shortly thereafter the two of them
made it safely to the other side. As the stranger slid
off the back of the horse onto dry ground, one in
the group asked him, "Tell me, why did you select
the president to ask this favor of?" The man was
shocked, admitting he had no idea it was the president who had helped him. "All I know," he said,
"is that on some of your faces was written the
answer 'No,' and on some of them was the answer
'Yes.' His was a 'Yes' face."[2]

Freedom gives people a "Yes" face. I am
confident Jesus had a "Yes" face. What a contrast
He must have been! He was surrounded by let-
tered men, religious, robed, *righteous*, law-quoting,

---

2. Ibid., 22.

professional men whose very demeanor announced "No!" Pious without, killers within . . . yet none of their poison seeped into His life. On the contrary, He revolutionized the entire direction of religion because He announced "Yes" while all His professional peers were frowning "No." How could it be? What was it that kept Him from getting caught in their grip? In one word, it was grace. He was so full of truth and grace, He left no inner space for their legalistic poison.

While thinking back on his days with Jesus, John (one of the Twelve) remembers there was something about Him that was like no one else, during which time His disciples "beheld His glory." His uniqueness was that incredible "glory," a glory that represented the very presence of God. In addition, this glorious One was "full of grace and truth." It was His glory mixed with grace and truth that made Him different. In a world of darkness and demands, rules and regulations, requirements and expectations demanded by the hypocritical religious leaders, Jesus came and ministered in a new and different way—He alone, full of grace and truth, introduced a revolutionary, different way of life.

Remembering that uniqueness, John adds, "For of His fullness we have all received, and grace upon grace" (John 1:16).

Don't miss the tie-in with John 1:14. Initially, John wrote, "We beheld His glory," and then he added, in effect, "We received His fullness." John and the other disciples became marked men as a result. Grace heaped upon grace rubbed off, leaving them different. His style became theirs. His tolerance, theirs. His acceptance, love, warmth, and compassion were absorbed by those men, so much so it ultimately transformed their lives. By the end of the first century, the ministry of those same men had sent shock waves throughout the Roman world.

John sums up the difference between contrastive styles of ministry: "For the Law was given through Moses; grace and truth were realized through Jesus Christ" (John 1:17). With the Mosaic Law came requirements, rules, regulations. With those exacting demands came galling expectations, which fueled the Pharisees' fire. By adding to the laws, the Pharisees not only lengthened the list, they intensified everyone's guilt and shame. Obsessed with duty, external conduct, and a constant focusing only on right and wrong (especially in others' lives), they promoted a system so demanding there was no room left for joy. This led to harsh, judgmental, even prejudicial pronouncements as the religious system they promoted degenerated into external performance rather than internal authenticity. Obedience became a matter of grim compulsion instead of a joyous overflow prompted by love.

But when "grace and truth were realized through Jesus Christ," a long-awaited revolution of the heart began to set religious captives free. Fearful

bondage motivated by guilt was replaced with a fresh
motivation to follow Him in truth simply out of
deep devotion and delight. The change spelled
freedom, as the Lord Himself taught: "You shall
know the truth, and the truth shall make you free"
(John 8:32). Rigid, barren religion was, at last,
replaced by a grace-oriented relationship—liberating grace. His followers loved it. His enemies hated
it . . . and Him.

Grace: Let's Understand the Term

What exactly is grace? And is it limited to
Jesus' life and ministry? You may be surprised to
know that Jesus never used the word. He just taught
it, and, equally important, He lived it.
Furthermore, the Bible never gives us a one-state-
ment definition, though grace appears throughout
its pages . . . not only the word itself but numerous
demonstrations of it. Understanding what grace
means requires our going back to an old Hebrew
term that meant "to bend, to stoop." By and by, it
came to include the idea of "condescending favor."

If you have traveled to London, you have perhaps seen royalty. If so, you may have noticed
sophistication, aloofness, distance. On occasion,
royalty in England will make the news because
someone in the ranks of nobility will stop, kneel
down, and touch or bless a commoner. That is
grace. There is nothing in the commoner that
deserves being noticed or touched or blessed by the

royal family. But because of grace in the heart of the royal person, there is the desire at that moment to pause, to stoop, to touch, even to bless.

The late pastor and Bible scholar Donald Barnhouse perhaps said it best: "Love that goes upward is worship; love that goes outward is affection; love that stoops is grace."[3]

To show grace is to extend favor or kindness to one who doesn't deserve it and can never earn it. Receiving God's acceptance by grace always stands in sharp contrast to earning it on the basis of works. Every time the thought of grace appears, there is the idea of its being undeserved. In no way is the recipient getting what he or she deserves. Favor is being extended simply out of the goodness of the heart of the giver.

One more thing should be emphasized about grace: It is absolutely and totally free. You will never be asked to pay it back. You couldn't even if you tried. Most of us have trouble with that thought, because we work for everything we get. As the old saying goes, "There ain't no free lunch." But in this case, grace comes to us free and clear, no strings attached. We should not even try to repay it; to do so is insulting.

Now that Christ has come and died and thereby satisfied the Father's demands on sin, all we need to do is claim His grace by accepting the free

3. Donald Grey Barnhouse, *Romans, Man's Ruin*, vol. 1 (Grand Rapids, Mich.: Wm. B. Eerdmans Publishing Company, 1952), 72.

gift of eternal life. Period. He smiles on us because of His Son's death and resurrection.

It's grace, my friend, amazing grace!

CHARLES R. SWINDOLL IS SENIOR PASTOR of Stonebriar Community Church, chancellor of Dallas Theological Seminary, and host of the internationally syndicated radio program *Insight for Living.* He has written more than 30 top-selling books, such as *Strengthening Your Grip, Laugh Again,* and the "Great Lives" series. Chuck and his wife, Cynthia, live in Dallas, TX.

THE GRACE AWAKENING
Hardcover, 304 pages
© 1990, 1996, 2003 by Charles R. Swindoll Inc.
W Publishing Group
ISBN: 0849918057

BIOGRAPHY

The Hiding Place

CORRIE TEN BOOM WITH
JOHN AND ELIZABETH SHERRILL

*The best-selling story of
how a Dutch watchmaker
became a heroine of
the WWII Resistance, a
survivor of Ravensbruck, and
a remarkable evangelist.*

"GOOD EVENING," HE SAID again.

"Evening."

He reached the street door and was gone. We had got away with it this time, but somehow, some way, we were going to have to work out a warning system.

For meanwhile, in the weeks since Mrs. Kleermaker's unexpected visit, a great deal had happened at the Beje. Supplied with ration cards, Mrs. Kleermaker and the elderly couple and the next arrivals and the next had found homes in safer locations. But still the hunted people kept coming, and the needs were often more complicated than rations cards and addresses. If a Jewish woman became pregnant where could she go to have her baby? If a Jew in hiding died, how could he be buried?

"Develop your own sources," Willem had said. And from the moment Fred Koornstra's name had popped into my mind, an uncanny realization had been growing in me. We were friends with half of Haarlem! We knew nurses in the maternity hospital. We knew clerks in the Records Office. We knew someone in every business and service in the city.

We didn't know, of course, the political views of all these people. But—and here I felt a strange leaping of my heart—God did! My job was simply to follow His leading one step at a time, holding every decision up to Him in prayer. I knew I was not clever or subtle or sophisticated; if the Beje was becoming a meeting place for need and supply, it was through some strategy far higher than mine.

A few nights after Fred's first "meterman" visit the alley bell rang long after curfew. I sped downstairs expecting another sad and stammering refugee. Betsie and I had already made up beds for four new overnight guests that evening: a Jewish woman and her three small children.

But to my surprise, close against the wall of
the dark alley, stood Kik. "Get your bicycle," he
ordered with his usual young abruptness. "And put
on a sweater. I have some people I want you to
meet."

"Now? After curfew?" But I knew it was use-
less to ask questions. Kik's bicycle was tireless too,
the wheel rims swathed in cloth. He wrapped mine
also to keep down the clatter, and soon we were ped-
aling through the blacked-out streets of Haarlem at
a speed that would have scared me even in daylight.

"Put a hand on my shoulder," Kik whispered.
"I know the way."

We crossed dark side streets, crested bridges,
wheeled round invisible corners. At last we crossed
a broad canal and I knew we had reached the fash-
ionable suburb of Aerdenhout.

We turned into a driveway beneath shadowy
trees. To my astonishment Kik picked up my bicycle
and carried both his and mine up the front steps. A
serving girl with starched white apron and ruffled
cap opened the door. The entrance hall was
jammed with bicycles.

Then I saw him. One eye smiling at me, the
other at the door, his vast stomach hastening ahead
of him. Pickwick!

He led Kik and me into the drawing room
where, sipping coffee and chatting in small groups,
was the most distinguished-looking group of men
and women I had ever seen. But all my attention,

that first moment, was on the inexpressibly fragrant aroma in that room. Surely, was it possible, they were drinking real coffee?

Pickwick drew me a cup from the silver urn on the sideboard. It was coffee. After two years, rich, black, pungent Dutch coffee. He poured himself a cup too, dropping in his usual five lumps of sugar as though rationing had never been invented. Another starched and ruffled maid was passing a tray heaped high with cakes.

Gobbling and gulping I trailed about the room after Pickwick, shaking the hands of the people he singled out. They were strange introductions for no names were mentioned, only, occasionally, an address, and "Ask for Mrs. Smit." When I had met my fourth Smit, Kik explained with a grin, "It's the only last name in the underground."

So this was really and truly the underground! But—where were these people from? I had never laid eyes on any of them. A second later I realized with a shiver down my spine that I was meeting the national group.

Their chief work, I gleaned from bits of conversation, was liaison with England and the Free Dutch forces fighting elsewhere on the continent. They also maintained the underground route through which downed Allied plane crews reached the North Sea coast.

But they were instantly sympathetic with my efforts to help Haarlem's Jews. I blushed to my hair roots to hear Pickwick describe me a "the head of an operation here in this city." A hollow space under the stairs and some haphazard friendships were not an operation. The others here were obviously competent, disciplined, and professional.

But they greeted me with grave courtesy, murmuring what they had to offer as we shook hands. False identity papers. The use of a car with official government plates. Signature forgery.

In a far corner of the room Pickwick introduced me to a frail-appearing little man with a wispy goatee. "Our host informs me," the little man began formally, "that your headquarters building lacks a secret room. This is a danger for all, those you are helping as well as yourselves and those who work with you. With your permission I will pay you a visit in the coming week. . . ."

Years later I learned that he was one of the most famous architects in Europe. I knew him only as Mr. Smit.

Just before Kik and I started our dash back to the Beje, Pickwick slipped an arm through mine. "My dear, I have good news. I understand that Peter is about to be released." . . .

So he was, three days later, thinner, paler, and not a whit daunted by his two months in a concrete cell. Nollie, Tine, and Betsie used up a month's sugar ration baking cakes for his welcome-home party.

And one morning soon afterward the first customer in the shop was a small thin-bearded man named Smit. Father took his jeweler's glass from his eye. If there was one thing he loved better than making a new acquaintance, it was discovering a link with an old one.

"Smit," he said eagerly. "I know several Smits in Amsterdam. Are you by any chance related to the family who _____ "

"Father," I interrupted, "This is the man I told you about. He's come to, ah, inspect the house."

"A building inspector? Then you must be the Smit with offices in the Grote Hout Straat. I wonder that I haven't _____ "

"Father!" I pleaded, "He's not a building inspector and his name is not Smit."

"Not Smit?"

Together Mr. Smit and I attempted to explain, but Father simply could not understand a person's being called by a name not his own. As I led Mr. Smit into the back hall we heard him musing to himself, "I once knew a Smit on Koning Straat. . . ."

Mr. Smit examined and approved the hiding place for ration cards beneath the bottom step. He also pronounced acceptable the warning system we had worked out. This was a triangle-shaped wooden sign advertising "Alpina Watches" which I had placed in the dining room window. As long as the sign was in place, it was safe to enter.

But when I showed him a cubby hole behind the corner cupboard in the dining room, he shook his head. Some ancient redesigning of the house had left a crawl space in that corner and we'd been secreting jewelry, silver coins, and other valuables there since the start of the occupation. Not only the rabbi had brought us his library but other Jewish families had brought their treasures to the Beje for safe-keeping. The space was large enough that we had believed a person could crawl in there if necessary, but Mr. Smit dismissed it without a second glance.

"First place they'd look. Don't bother to change it though. It's only silver. We're interested in saving people, not things."

He started up the narrow corkscrew stairs, and as he mounted so did his spirits. He paused in delight at the odd-placed landings, pounded on the crooked walls, and laughed aloud as the floor levels of the two old houses continued out of phase.

"What an impossibility!" he said in an awestruck voice. "What an improbable, unbelievable, unpredictable impossibility! Miss ten Boom, if all houses were constructed like this one, you would see before you a less worried man."

At last, at the very top of the stairs, he entered my room and gave a little cry of delight. "This is it!" he exclaimed.

"You want your hiding place as high as

possible," he went on eagerly. "Gives you the best chance to reach it while the search is on below. He leaned out the window, craning his thin neck, the little faun's beard pointing this way and that.

"But . . . this is my bedroom. . . ."

Mr. Smit paid no attention. He was already measuring. He moved the heavy, wobbly old wardrobe away from the wall with surprising ease and pulled my bed into the center of the room. "This is where the false wall will go!" Excitedly he drew out a pencil and drew a line along the floor thirty inches from the back wall. He stood up and gazed at it moodily.

"That's a big as I dare," he said. "It will take a cot mattress, though. Oh yes. Easily!"

I tried again to protest, but Mr. Smit had forgotten I existed. Over the next few days he and his workmen were in and out of our house constantly. They never knocked. At each visit each man carried in something. Tools in a folded newspaper. A few bricks in a briefcase. "Wood!" he exclaimed when I ventured to wonder if a wooden wall would not be easier to build. "Wood sounds hollow. Hear it in a minute. No, no. Brick's the only thing for false walls."

After the wall was up, the plasterer came, then the carpenter, finally the painter. Six days after he had begun, Mr. Smit called Father, Betsie, and me to see.

We stood in the doorway and gaped. The

smell of fresh paint was everywhere. But surely
nothing in this room was newly painted! All four
walls had that streaked and grimy look that old
rooms got in coal-burning Haarlem. The ancient
molding ran unbroken around the ceiling,
chipped and peeling here and there, obviously
undisturbed for a hundred and fifty years. Old
water stains streaked the back wall, a wall that even I
who had lived half a century in this room, could
scarcely believe was not the original, but set back a
precious two-and-a-half feet from the true wall of
the building.

Built-in bookshelves ran along this false wall,
old, sagging shelves whose blistered wood bore the
same water stains as the wall behind them. Down in
the far lefthand corner, beneath the bottom shelf, a
sliding panel, two feet high and two wide, opened
into the secret room.

Mr. Smit stooped and silently pulled this
panel up. On hands and knees Betsie and I crawled
into the narrow room behind it. Once inside we
could stand up, sit, or even stretch out one at a
time on the single mattress. A concealed vent, cun-
ningly let into the real wall, allowed air to enter
from outside.

"Keep a water jug there," said Mr. Smit,
crawling in behind us. "Change the water once a
week. Hardtack and vitamins keep indefinitely.
Anytime there is anyone in the house whose presence is unofficial, all possessions except the clothes

actually on his back must be stored in here."

Dropping to our knees again we crawled single file out into my bedroom. "Move back into this room," he told me. "Everything exactly as before."

With his fist he struck the wall above the bookshelves.

"The Gestapo could search for a year," he said. "They'll never find this one." ✗

———————

CORRIE TEN BOOM (1892-1983) WAS imprisoned by the Nazis and endured 10 months in Ravensbruck for hiding Jews in her family home in Holland. After her release at age 52, Corrie spoke around the world and wrote several books, including *Tramp for the Lord* and *In My Father's House.*

JOHN AND ELIZABETH SHERRILL HAVE co-authored numerous top-sellers, including *The Cross and the Switchblade,* and have traveled the world researching and writing articles and books. Former senior editors and now roving editors for *Guideposts,* they co-founded Chosen Books with Leonard and Catherine Marshall LeSourd.

THE HIDING PLACE (25TH ANNIVERSARY EDITION)
Paper, 221 pages
© 1971 and 1984 by Corrie ten Boom and John and Elizabeth Sherrill
Chosen Books, a division of Baker Publishing Group
ISBN: 0-8007-9247-5

Atention participating CBA Member Store: For refund of this coupon minus a handling fee, return all original coupons to CBA Sampler, P.O. Box 62000, Colorado Springs, CO 80962-2000. All coupons for this promotion must be returned in the same envelope no later than October 15, 2004. Only one refund per store will be issued for this promotion.

Coupon redeemed at:

Date: _____

Atention participating CBA Member Store: For refund of this coupon minus a handling fee, return all original coupons to CBA Sampler, P.O. Box 62000, Colorado Springs, CO 80962-2000. All coupons for this promotion must be returned in the same envelope no later than October 15, 2004. Only one refund per store will be issued for this promotion.

Coupon redeemed at:

Date: _____

Atention participating CBA Member Store: For refund of this coupon minus a handling fee, return all original coupons to CBA Sampler, P.O. Box 62000, Colorado Springs, CO 80962-2000. All coupons for this promotion must be returned in the same envelope no later than October 15, 2004. Only one refund per store will be issued for this promotion.

Coupon redeemed at:

Date: _____

Atention participating CBA Member Store: For refund of this coupon minus a handling fee, return all original coupons to CBA Sampler, P.O. Box 62000, Colorado Springs, CO 80962-2000. All coupons for this promotion must be returned in the same envelope no later than October 15, 2004. Only one refund per store will be issued for this promotion.

Coupon redeemed at:

Date: _____

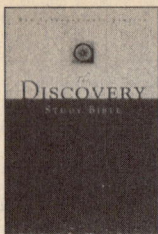

$2 OFF!

NIV Discovery Study Bible

Redeem this coupon for $2 off the regular retail price.

Offer good only at the store that provided this sampler. Limit one coupon per book, one book per coupon. Coupon cannot be copied or combined with other offers or discounts.

Expiration date: September 30, 2004.

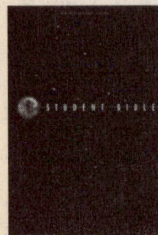

$2 OFF!

NIV Prayer Devotional Bible

Redeem this coupon for $2 off the regular retail price.

Offer good only at the store that provided this sampler. Limit one coupon per book, one book per coupon. Coupon cannot be copied or combined with other offers or discounts.

Expiration date: September 30, 2004.

$2 OFF!

NIV Quest Study Bible

Redeem this coupon for $2 off the regular retail price.

Offer good only at the store that provided this sampler. Limit one coupon per book, one book per coupon. Coupon cannot be copied or combined with other offers or discounts.

Expiration date: September 30, 2004.

$2 OFF!

NIV Student Bible

Redeem this coupon for $2 off the regular retail price.

Offer good only at the store that provided this sampler. Limit one coupon per book, one book per coupon. Coupon cannot be copied or combined with other offers or discounts.

Expiration date: September 30, 2004.

∽ BIBLE/GENERAL ∽
VERSIONS/TRANSLATIONS

NIV Study Bible

*The No. 1 best-selling
study Bible in the
most-read,
most-trusted
NIV Translation.*

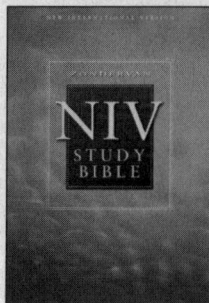

NIV Study Bible
Hardcover and Leather, 2,240 pages
© 1985, 1995, 2002 by Zondervan

Colossians

INTRODUCTION

Author, Date and Place of Writing

That Colossians is a genuine letter of Paul (1:1) is usually not disputed. In the early church, all who speak on the subject of authorship ascribe it to Paul. In the 19th century, however, some thought that the heresy refuted in ch. 2 was second-century Gnosticism. But a careful analysis of ch. 2 shows that the heresy referred to there is noticeably less developed than the Gnosticism of leading Gnostic teachers of the second and third centuries. Also, the seeds of what later became the full-blown Gnosticism of the second century were present in the first century and already making inroads into the churches. Consequently, it is not necessary to date Colossians in the second century at a time too late for Paul to have written the letter.

Instead, it is to be dated during Paul's first imprisonment in Rome, where he spent at least two years under house arrest (see Ac 28:16–31). Some have argued that Paul wrote Colossians from Ephesus or Caesarea, but most of the evidence favors Rome as the place where Paul penned all the Prison Letters (Ephesians, Colossians, Philippians and Philemon). Colossians should be dated c. A.D. 60, in the same year as Ephesians and Philemon (see chart, p. 2261).

Colosse: The Town and the Church

Several hundred years before Paul's day, Colosse had been a leading city in Asia Minor (present-day Turkey). It was located on the Lycus River and on the great east-west trade route leading from Ephesus on the Aegean Sea to the Euphrates River (see map, p. 2288). By the first century A.D. Colosse was diminished to a second-rate market town, which had been surpassed long before in power and importance by the neighboring towns of Laodicea and Hierapolis (see 4:13).

What gave Colosse NT importance, however, was the fact that, during Paul's three-year ministry in Ephesus, Epaphras had been converted and had carried the gospel to Colosse (cf. 1:7–8; Ac 19:10). The young church that resulted then became the target of heretical attack, which led to Epaphras's visit to Paul in Rome and ultimately to the penning of the Colossian letter.

Perhaps as a result of the efforts of Epaphras or other converts of Paul, Christian churches had also been established in Laodicea and Hierapolis. Some of them were house churches (see 4:15; Phm 2). Most likely all of them were primarily Gentile.

The Colossian Heresy

Paul never explicitly describes the false teaching he opposes in the Colossian letter. The nature of the heresy must be inferred from statements he made in opposition to the false teachers. An analysis of his refutation suggests that the heresy was diverse in nature. Some of the elements of its teachings were:

1. *Ceremonialism.* It held to strict rules about the kinds of permissible food and drink, religious festivals (2:16–17) and circumcision (2:11; 3:11).
2. *Asceticism.* "Do not handle! Do not taste! Do not touch!" (2:21; cf. 2:23).

3. *Angel worship.* See 2:18.

4. *Depreciation of Christ.* This is implied in Paul's emphasis on the supremacy of Christ (1:15–20; 2:2–3,9).

5. *Secret knowledge.* The Gnostics boasted of this (see 2:18 and Paul's emphasis in 2:2–3 on Christ, "in whom are hidden all the treasures of wisdom").

6. *Reliance on human wisdom and tradition.* See 2:4,8.

These elements seem to fall into two categories, Jewish and Gnostic. It is likely, therefore, that the Colossian heresy was a mixture of an extreme form of Judaism and an early stage of Gnosticism (see Introduction to 1 John: Gnosticism; see also note on 2:23).

Purpose and Theme

Paul's purpose is to refute the Colossian heresy. To accomplish this goal, he exalts Christ as the very image of God (1:15), the Creator (1:16), the preexistent sustainer of all things (1:17), the head of the church (1:18), the first to be resurrected (1:18), the fullness of deity in bodily form (1:19; 2:9) and the reconciler (1:20–22). Thus Christ is completely adequate. We "have been given fullness in Christ" (2:10). On the other hand, the Colossian heresy was altogether inadequate. It was a hollow and deceptive philosophy (2:8), lacking any ability to restrain the old sinful nature (2:23).

The theme of Colossians is the complete adequacy of Christ as contrasted with the emptiness of mere human philosophy.

Outline

I. Introduction (1:1–14)
   A. Greetings (1:1–2)
   B. Thanksgiving (1:3–8)
   C. Prayer (1:9–14)
II. The Supremacy of Christ (1:15–23)
III. Paul's Labor for the Church (1:24—2:7)
   A. His Ministry for the Sake of the Church (1:24–29)
   B. His Concern for the Spiritual Welfare of His Readers (2:1–7)
IV. Freedom from Human Regulations through Life with Christ (2:8–23)
   A. Warning to Guard against the False Teachers (2:8–15)
   B. Pleas to Reject the False Teachers (2:16–19)
   C. An Analysis of the Heresy (2:20–23)
V. Rules for Holy Living (3:1—4:6)
   A. The Old Self and the New Self (3:1–17)
   B. Rules for Christian Households (3:18—4:1)
   C. Further Instructions (4:2–6)
VI. Final Greetings and Benediction (4:7–18)

COLOSSIANS 1:1

1 Paul, an apostle[a] of Christ Jesus by the will of God,[b] and Timothy[c] our brother,

[2] To the holy and faithful[a] brothers in Christ at Colosse:

Grace[d] and peace to you from God our Father.[b.e]

Thanksgiving and Prayer

[3] We always thank God,[f] the Father of our Lord Jesus Christ, when we pray for you, [4] because we have heard of your faith in Christ Jesus and of the love[g] you have for all the saints[h]— [5] the faith and love that spring from the hope[i] that is stored up for you in heaven[j] and that you have already heard about in the word of truth,[k] the gospel [6] that has come to you. All over the world[l] this gospel is bearing fruit[m] and

growing, just as it has been doing among you since the day you heard it and understood God's grace in all its truth. [7] You learned it from Epaphras,[n] our dear fellow servant, who is a faithful minister[o] of Christ on our[e] behalf, [8] and who also told us of your love in the Spirit.[p]

[9] For this reason, since the day we heard about you,[q] we have not stopped praying for you[r] and asking God to fill you with the knowledge of his will[s] through all spiritual wisdom and understanding.[t] [10] And we pray this in order that you may live a life worthy[u] of the Lord and may please him[v] in every way: bearing fruit in every good work, growing in the knowledge of

1:1	*5 1Co 1:1
	*5 2Co 1:1
	*5 Ac 16:1
1:2	*Col 4:18
	*5 Ro 1:7
1:3	*5 Ro 1:8
1:4	*Col 5:6
	*5 Ac 9:13;
	Eph 1:15; Phm 5
1:5	*ver 23;
	1Th 5:8; Tit 1:2
	*1Pe 1:4
	*5 2Ti 2:15
1:6	*ver 23;
	5 Ro 10:18
	*Jn 15:16

1:7	*Col 4:12;
	Phm 23 *Col 4:7
1:8	*Ro 15:30
1:9	*ver 4;
	Eph 1:15
	*5 Ro 1:10
	*5 Eph 5:17
	*5 Eph 1:17
1:10	*5 Eph 4:1
	*5 2Co 5:9

*a 2 Or believing   *b 2 Some manuscripts Father and the Lord Jesus Christ   *c 7 Some manuscripts your*

1:1 *Paul.* It was customary to put the writer's name at the beginning of a letter. For more information on Paul see note on Ro 1:1. *apostle . . . by the will of God.* See 1Co 1:1 and note. *Christ.* Paul is very Christ-centered, as seen by this short letter, in which he uses the title "Christ" 29 times and the title "Lord" (alone) 9 times. *Timothy.* Paul also mentions Timothy in 2 Corinthians, Philippians, 1,2 Thessalonians and Philemon, but Paul is really the sole author, as seen by the constant use of the pronoun "I" (see especially 4:18).

1:2 *holy.* Because of Christ's substitutionary death for the Colossian believers, they are declared holy in the sight of God, and because of the Holy Spirit's work, they are continuing to be made holy in their lives (see notes on Ro 1:7; 6:22; 1Co 1:2. *faithful.* See 1:7; 4:7,9. *brothers.* See note on Ro 1:13. *in Christ.* Paul mentions the spiritual union with Christ 12 times in Colossians (see note on Eph 1:1). *Grace and peace.* See note on Ro 1:7.

1:3 *We.* Paul and Timothy (v. 1). *thank God.* Every one of Paul's letters, except Galatians, begins with thanks or praise (see note on Php 1:3–4). In Colossians thanks is an important theme (see v. 12; 2:7; 3:15–17; 4:2). In the Bible humans are never thanked for their faith and love, but rather God, who is the source of these virtues.

1:4 *saints.* See note on Ro 1:7.

1:5 The three great Christian virtues of faith, love and hope appear also in Ro 5:2–5; 1Co 13:13; Gal 5:5–6; 1Th 1:3; 5:8; Heb 10:22–24. *hope.* Not wishful thinking but a firm assurance (see Ro 5:5 and note). For this unusual thought of faith and love com-

ing from hope see Tit 1:2. *word of truth.* The "gospel" (see Eph 1:13; 2Ti 2:15).

1:6 *All over the world.* Hyperbole, to dramatize the rapid spread of the gospel into every quarter of the Roman empire within three decades of Pentecost (see v. 23; Ro 1:8 and note; 10:18; 16:19). In refutation of the charge of the false teachers, Paul insists that the Christian faith is not merely local or regional but worldwide.

1:7 *Epaphras.* A native (4:12) and probably founder of the Colossian church, and an evangelist in nearby Laodicea and Hierapolis (4:13). Paul loved and admired him, calling him a "fellow prisoner" (Phm 23), his "dear fellow servant" and "a faithful minister of Christ." Epaphras was the one who told Paul at Rome about the Colossian church problem and thereby stimulated him to write this letter (vv. 4,8). His name, a shortened form of Epaphroditus (from "Aphrodite," the Greek goddess of love), suggests that he was a convert from paganism. He is not the Epaphroditus of Php 2:25; 4:18.

1:8 *your love in the Spirit.* The Holy Spirit is the source of all Christian love (see Ro 5:5; Gal 5:22–23 and notes).

1:9 *knowledge of his will.* Biblical knowledge is not merely the possession of facts. Rather, knowledge and wisdom in the Bible are practical, having to do with godly living. This is borne out by vv. 10–12, where knowledge, wisdom and understanding result in a life worthy of the Lord.

1:10 *live a life.* This phrase (lit. "walk") is linked to 2:7; 3:7; 4:5 ("act") by the same Greek verb. *bearing fruit . . . growing.* Cf. v. 6.

God,[w] 11being strengthened with all power[x] according to his glorious might so that you may have great endurance and patience,[y] and joyfully 12giving thanks to the Father,[z] who has qualified you[a] to share in the inheritance[a] of the saints in the kingdom of light.[b] 13For he has rescued us from the dominion of darkness[c] and brought us into the kingdom[d] of the Son he loves,[e] 14in whom we have redemption,[b][f] the forgiveness of sins.[g]

The Supremacy of Christ

15He is the image[h] of the invisible God,[i] the firstborn[j] over all creation. 16For by him all things were created:[k] things in heaven and on earth, visible and invisible, wheth-

1:10	[w]ver 6
1:11	[x]S Php 4:13
	[y]Eph 4:2
1:12	[z]Eph 5:20
	[a]S Ac 20:32
	[b]S Ac 26:18
1:13	[c]S Ac 26:18
	[d]2Pe 1:11 [:]Mt 3:17
1:14	[e]S Ro 3:24
	[b]Eph 1:7
1:15	[h]S Jn 14:9
	[i]S Jn 1:18; 1Ti 1:17;
	Heb 11:27
	[j]S ver 18
1:16	[k]S Jn 1:3

1:16	[l]Eph 1:20,21
	[m]S Ro 11:36
1:17	[n]S Jn 1:2
1:18	[o]S Eph 1:22
	[p]ver 24;
	S 1Co 12:27
	[q]ver 15; Ps 89:27;
	Ro 8:29; Heb 1:6
	[*]Ac 26:23; Rev 1:5
1:19	[s]S Eph 1:5
	[t]S Jn 1:16
1:20	[u]S Ro 5:10
	[v]Eph 1:10
	[w]S Lk 2:14
	[x]Eph 2:13

er thrones or powers or rulers or authorities;[l] all things were created by him and for him.[m] 17He is before all things,[n] and in him all things hold together. 18And he is the head[o] of the body, the church;[p] he is the beginning and the firstborn[q] from among the dead,[r] so that in everything he might have the supremacy. 19For God was pleased[s] to have all his fullness[t] dwell in him, 20and through him to reconcile[u] to himself all things, whether things on earth or things in heaven,[v] by making peace[w] through his blood,[x] shed on the cross.

21Once you were alienated from God and were enemies[y] in your

a 12 Some manuscripts us   b 14 A few late manuscripts redemption through his blood

1:12 inheritance. See 1Pe 1:4 and note. light. Often symbolizes holiness (see 1Jn 1:5 and note), truth (Ps 119:105,130; 2Co 4:6), glory (Isa 60:1–3; 1Ti 6:16) and life (Jn 1:4). Accordingly, God (1Jn 1:5), Christ (Jn 8:12) and the Christian (Eph 5:8) are characterized by light. The "kingdom of light" is the opposite of the "dominion of darkness" (v. 13). See also note on Ps 27:1.

1:13 kingdom. Does not here refer to a territory but to the authority, rule or sovereign power of a king. Here it means that the Christian is no longer under the dominion of evil (darkness) but under the benevolent rule of God's Son.

1:14 redemption. Deliverance and freedom from the penalty of sin by the payment of a ransom—the substitutionary death of Christ (see Ro 3:24 and note).

1:15–20 Perhaps an early Christian hymn (see note on 3:16) on the supremacy of Christ—used here by Paul to counteract the false teaching at Colosse. It is divided into two parts: (1) Christ's supremacy in creation (vv. 15–17); (2) Christ's supremacy in redemption (vv. 18–20).

1:15 image. Christ is called the "image of God" here and in 2Co 4:4 (see note there). In Heb 1:3 he is described as the "radiance of God's glory and the exact representation of his being." This figure of the image suggests two truths: (1) God is invisible ("No one has ever seen God," Jn 1:18); (2) Christ, who is the eternal Son of God and who became the God-man, reflects and reveals him (see also Jn 1:18; 14:9). firstborn over all creation. Just as the firstborn son had certain privileges and rights in the Biblical world, so also Christ has certain rights in relation to all creation—priority, preeminence and sovereignty (vv. 16–18).

1:16 by him all things were created. See Jn 1:3. Seven times in vv. 15–20 Paul mentions "all creation," "all things" and "everything," thus stressing that Christ is supreme over all. thrones or powers or rulers or authorities. Angels. An angelic hierarchy figured prominently in the Colossian heresy (see Introduction: The Colossian Heresy).

1:17 He is before all things. Referring to time, as in Jn 1:1–2; 8:58.

1:18 head. Christ is supreme in the church as the one on whom it is dependent (see notes on 1Co 11:3; Eph 1:22). beginning. Of the new creation. firstborn. Christ was the first to rise from the dead with a resurrection body. Elsewhere Paul calls him the "firstfruits of those who have fallen asleep" (1Co 15:20). Others who were raised from the dead (2Ki 4:35; Lk 7:15; Jn 11:44; Ac 9:36–41; 20:7–12) were raised only to die again.

1:19 fullness. Part of the technical vocabulary of some Gnostic philosophies. In these systems it meant the sum of the supernatural forces controlling the fate of people. For Paul "fullness" meant the totality of God with all his powers and attributes (see 2:9 and note).

1:20 reconcile to himself all things. Does not mean that Christ by his death has saved all people. Scripture speaks of an eternal hell and makes clear that only believers are saved. When Adam and Eve sinned, not only was the harmony between God and human beings destroyed, but also disorder came into creation (Ro 8:19–22). So when Christ died on the cross, he made peace possible between God and humans, and he restored in principle the harmony in the physical world, though the full realization of the minds[z] because of[a] your evil behavior. [22]But now he has reconciled[a] you by Christ's physical body[b] through death to present you[c] holy in his sight, without blemish and free from accusation[d]— [23]if you continue[e] in your faith, established[f] and firm, not moved from the hope[g] held out in the gospel. This is the gospel that you heard and that has been proclaimed to every creature under heaven,[h] and of which I, Paul, have become a servant.[i]

Paul's Labor for the Church

[24]Now I rejoice[j] in what was suffered for you, and I fill up in my flesh what is still lacking in regard to Christ's afflictions,[k] for the sake of his body, which is the church.[l] [25]I have become its servant[m] by the commission God gave me[n] to present to you the word of God[o] in its fullness— [26]the mystery[p] that has been kept hidden for ages and generations, but is now disclosed to the saints. [27]To them God has chosen to make known[q] among the Gentiles the glorious riches[r] of this mystery, which is Christ in you,[s] the hope of glory.

[28]We proclaim him, admonishing[t] and teaching everyone with all wisdom,[u] so that we may present everyone perfect[v] in Christ. [29]To this end I labor,[w] struggling[x] with all his energy, which so powerfully works in me.[y]

2 I want you to know how much I am struggling[z] for you and for those at Laodicea,[a] and for all who have not met me personally. [2]My purpose is that they may be encouraged in heart[b] and united in love, so that they may have the full riches of complete understanding, in order that they may know the

a 21 Or minds, as shown by

1:21	/Ro 5:10
	fEph 2:3
1:22	ª ver 26;
	S Ro 5:10 ªRo 7:4
	³S 2Co 4:14
	ᵇEph 1:4;5:27
1:23	²S Ro 11:22
	fEph 3:17 ªver 5
	ʰver 6; S Ro 10:18
	ʲver 25; S 1Co 3:5
1:24	ᵏS 2Co 6:10
	ˡS 2Co 1:5
	ˡS 1Co 12:27
1:25	ᵐver 23;
	S 1Co 3:5 ⁿEph 3:2
1:25	ᵒS Heb 4:12
1:26	ᵖS Ro 16:25
1:27	ʳS Mt 13:11
	ˢRo 2:4
	ˢS Ro 8:10
1:28	ᵗCol 3:16
	ᵘ1Co 2:6,7
	ᵛMt 5:48;Eph 5:27
1:29	ʷ1Co 15:10;
	2Co 11:23 ˣCol 2:1
2:1	ᶻEph 1:19;3:7
	ᶻCol 1:29;4:12
	ªCol 4:13,15,16;
	Rev 1:11;3:14
2:2	ᵇEph 6:22;
	Col 4:8

---

latter will come only when Christ returns (see Ro 8:21 and note).

1:22 *death.* Christ's death.

1:23 *every creature.* See note on v. 6.

🔲 **1:24** *what was suffered.* By Paul. During his mission to the Gentiles, he experienced all kinds of affliction (see 2Co 11:23–27), but here he was probably referring especially to his imprisonment. *fill up . . . what is still lacking.* Does not mean that there was a deficiency in the atoning sacrifice of Christ. Rather, it means that Paul suffered afflictions because he was preaching the good news of Christ's atonement. Christ suffered on the cross to atone for sin, and Paul filled up Christ's afflictions by experiencing the added sufferings necessary to carry this good news to a lost world.

🔲 **1:25** *commission.* The task with which he was entrusted (see 1Co 9:17). *to present . . . the word of God in its fullness.* The meaning seems to be that the word of God is brought to completion, i.e., to its intended purpose, only when it is proclaimed (cf. Isa 55:11). Paul's commission to bring the word to completion, therefore, applied to make the word of God heard in Colosse as well as elsewhere. See Ro 15:19 for a similar statement.

1:26 *mystery.* The purpose of God, unknown to humans except by revelation. This word was a popular, pagan religious term, used in the mystery religions to refer to secret information available only to an exclusive group of people. Paul changes that meaning radically by always combining it with words such as "disclosed" (here), "made known" (Eph 1:9), "make plain" (Eph 3:9) and "revelation" (Ro 16:25; see note there). The Christian mystery is not secret knowledge for a few. It is a revelation of divine truths—once hidden but now openly proclaimed.

1:27 *Gentiles . . . Christ in you.* The mystery is the fact that Christ indwells Gentiles, for it had not been previously revealed that the Gentiles would be admitted to the church on equal terms with Israel (see note on Eph 3:6). *glory.* The glorious future prepared by God for his people (see 3:4; Ro 5:2 and note; 8:17–18; 1Co 2:7 and note; 15:42–44 and note; 2Co 4:17 and note; 1Th 2:12; 2Th 2:14; 2Ti 2:10; Heb 2:10; 1Pe 5:1 and note, 4).

1:28 *perfect.* Or "fully mature"; employed by the mystery religions and the Gnostics to describe those who had become possessors of the secrets or knowledge boasted of by the particular religion (see Introduction to 1 John: Gnosticism). But in Christ every believer is one of the "perfect" (or mature).

1:29 An example of the combination of human effort and divine help (see Php 2:12–13).

2:1 *I am struggling.* Probably a reference to Paul's prayers and inner conflicts and concerns for the Colossians. *Laodicea.* This letter was to be read to the church there too (4:16). Laodicea (near modern Denizli) was only about 11 miles from Colosse (see map 3, p. 2268).

2:2 *mystery.* See notes on 1:26; Ro 11:25.

mystery[c] of God, namely, Christ, [3]in whom are hidden all the treasures of wisdom and knowledge.[d] [4]I tell you this so that no one may deceive you by fine-sounding arguments.[e] [5]For though I am absent from you in body, I am present with you in spirit[f] and delight to see how orderly[g] you are and how firm[h] your faith in Christ[i] is.

Freedom From Human Regulations Through Life With Christ

[6]So then, just as you received Christ Jesus as Lord,[j] continue to live in him, [7]rooted[k] and built up in him, strengthened in the faith as you were taught,[l] and overflowing with thankfulness.

[8]See to it that no one takes you captive through hollow and deceptive philosophy,[m] which depends on human tradition and the basic principles of this world[n] rather than on Christ.

[9]For in Christ all the fullness[o] of the Deity lives in bodily form, [10]and you have been given fullness in Christ, who is the head[p] over every power and authority.[q] [11]In him you were also circumcised,[r] in the putting off of the sinful nature,[as] not with a circumcision done by the hands of men but with the circumcision done by Christ, [12]having been buried with him in baptism[t] and raised with him[u] through your faith in the power of God, who raised him from the dead.[v]

[13]When you were dead in your sins[w] and in the uncircumcision of your sinful nature,[b] God made you[c] alive[x] with Christ. He forgave us all our sins,[y] [14]having canceled the written code, with its regulations,[z] that was against us and that stood opposed to us; he took it away, nailing it to the cross.[a] [15]And having disarmed the powers and authorities,[b] he made a public spectacle of them, triumphing over them[c] by the cross.[a]

[a] 11 Or the flesh   [b] 13 Or your flesh   [c] 13 Some manuscripts us

---

2:2 [s] Ro 16:25
2:3 [r] Isa 11:2; Jer 23:5; Ro 11:33; 1Co 1:24,30
2:4 [s] Ro 16:18
2:5 [t] 1Co 5:4; 1Th 2:17
[u] 1Co 14:40
[v] 1Pe 5:9
[w] Ac 20:21
2:6 [s] Jn 13:13; Col 1:10
2:7 [b] Eph 3:17
[l] Eph 4:21
2:8 [m] 1Ti 6:20
[n] ver 20; Gal 4:3

2:9 [s] Jn 1:16
2:10 [p] Eph 1:22
[q] Mt 28:18
2:11 [r] Ro 2:29; Php 3:3; 1Gal 5:24
2:12 [s] Mt 28:19
[t] Ro 6:5
[u] Ac 2:24
2:13 [w] Eph 2:1,5
[x] Eph 2:5; Eph 4:32
2:14 [y] Eph 2:15
[z] Php 2:24
2:15 [b] ver 10; Eph 6:12

2:3 *knowledge.* Paul stressed knowledge in this letter (v. 2; 1:9–10) because he was refuting a heresy that emphasized knowledge as the means of salvation (see Introduction to 1 John: Gnosticism). Paul insisted that the Christian, not the Gnostic, possessed genuine knowledge.

2:5 *absent . . . in body, . . . present . . . in spirit.* Cf. 1Co 5:3.

2:6–7 Cf. Eph 3:16–19.

2:6 *live in him.* The believer's intimate, spiritual, living union with Christ is mentioned repeatedly in this letter (see, e.g., vv. 7,10–13,20; 1:2,27–28; 3:1,3).

2:7 *overflowing with thankfulness.* See Eph 5:20 and note.

2:8 *basic principles of this world.* This term (which occurs also in v. 20; Gal 4:3,9) means false, worldly, religious, elementary teachings. Paul was counteracting the Colossian heresy, which, in part, taught that for salvation one needed to combine faith in Christ with secret knowledge and with human regulations concerning such physical and external practices as circumcision, eating and drinking, and observance of religious festivals.

2:9 *fullness of the Deity.* See note on 1:19. The declaration that the very essence of deity was present in totality in Jesus' human body was a direct

refutation of Gnostic teaching.

2:10–15 Here Paul declares that the Christian is complete in Christ, rather than being deficient as the Gnostics claimed. This completeness includes the putting off of the sinful nature (v. 11), resurrection from spiritual death (vv. 12–13), forgiveness (v. 13) and deliverance from legalistic requirements (v. 14) and from evil spirit beings (v. 15).

2:10 *head.* Cf. 1:18 and note; see Eph 1:19–22 and notes.

2:11–12 *circumcision . . . baptism.* In the Israelite faith, circumcision was a sign that the individual stood in covenant relation with God. While this is the only reference where circumcision is associated with baptism, some see the passage as implying that, for the Christian, water baptism is the parallel sign of the covenant relationship.

2:12 See Ro 6:3–4 and notes.

2:13 Cf. Eph 2:1–9 and notes.

2:14 *written code.* A business term, meaning a certificate of indebtedness in the debtor's handwriting. Paul uses it as a designation for the Mosaic law, with all its regulations, under which everyone is a debtor to God.

2:15 *having disarmed.* Not only did God cancel out the accusations of the law against the Christian, but he also conquered and disarmed the evil angels

COLOSSIANS 2:16

[16]Therefore do not let anyone judge you[d] by what you eat or drink,[e] or with regard to a religious festival,[f] a New Moon celebration[g] or a Sabbath day.[h] [17]These are a shadow of the things that were to come;[i] the reality, however, is found in Christ. [18]Do not let anyone who delights in false humility[j] and the worship of angels disqualify you for the prize.[k] Such a person goes into great detail about what he has seen, and his unspiritual mind puffs him up with idle notions. [19]He has lost connection with the Head,[l] from whom the whole body,[m] supported and held together by its ligaments and sinews, grows as God causes it to grow.[n]

[20]Since you died with Christ[o] to the basic principles of this world,[p] why, as though you still belonged to it, do you submit to its rules:[q] [21]"Do not handle! Do not taste! Do not touch!"? [22]These are all destined to perish[r] with use, because they are based on human commands and teachings.[s] [23]Such regulations indeed have an appearance of wisdom, with their self-imposed worship, their false humility[t] and their harsh treatment of the body, but they lack any value in restraining sensual indulgence.

Rules for Holy Living

3 Since, then, you have been raised with Christ,[u] set your hearts on things above, where Christ is seated at the right hand of God.[v] [2]Set your minds on things above, not on earthly things.[w] [3]For

a 15 Or them in him

2:15	[c]Mt 12:29; Lk 10:18; Jn 12:31
2:16	[d]Ro 14:3,4
	[e]Mk 7:19; Ro 14:17
	[f]Lev 23:2; Ro 14:5
	[g]1Ch 23:31
	[h]Ne 2:27,28; Gal 4:10
2:17	[i]Heb 8:5; 10:1
2:18	[j]ver 23
	[k]1Co 9:24; Php 3:14
2:19	[l]S Eph 1:22
	[m]S 1Co 12:27
	[n]Eph 4:16
2:20	[o]S Ro 6:6
2:20	[p]ver 8; Gal 4:3,9;ver 14, 16
2:22	[q]1Co 6:13
	[r]Isa 29:13; Mt 15:9; Tit 1:14
2:23	[t]ver 18
3:1	[u]S Ro 6:5

(powers and authorities, 1:16; Eph 6:12), who entice people to follow asceticism and false teachings about Christ. The picture is of conquered soldiers stripped of their clothes as well as their weapons to symbolize their total defeat. *triumphing over them.* Lit. "leading them in a triumphal procession." The metaphor recalls a Roman general leading his captives through the streets of his city for all the citizens to see as evidence of his complete victory (see 2Co 2:14 and note). That Christ triumphed over the devil and his cohorts is seen from Mt 12:29; Lk 10:18; Ro 16:20.

2:16 Cf. Paul's exhortations to the Roman church (Ro 14:1—15:13).

2:17 *shadow . . . reality.* The ceremonial laws of the OT are here referred to as shadows (cf. Heb 8:5; 10:1) because they symbolically depicted the coming of Christ; so any insistence on the observance of such ceremonies is a failure to recognize that their fulfillment has already taken place. This element of the Colossian heresy was combined with a rigid asceticism, as vv. 20–21 reveal.

2:18 *false humility.* Humility in which one delights is of necessity mock humility. Paul may be referring to a professed humility in view of the absolute God, who was believed to be so far above humans that he could only be worshiped in the form of angels he had created. Second-century Gnosticism conceived of a list of spirit beings who had emanated from God and through whom God may be approached. *disqualify.* This term pictures an umpire or referee who excludes from competition any athlete who fails to follow the rules. The Colossians were not to permit any false teacher to deny the reality of their salvation because

they were not delighting in mock humility and in the worship of angelic beings. *what he has seen.* Probably refers to professed visions by the false teachers.

2:19 *lost connection with the Head.* The central error of the Colossian heresy is a defective view of Christ, in which he is believed to be less than deity (see v. 9; 1:19).

2:20 *basic principles.* See note on v. 8.

2:21 *Do not handle . . . taste . . . touch!* The strict ascetic nature of the heresy is seen here. These prohibitions seem to carry OT ceremonial laws to the extreme.

2:23 A rather detailed analysis of the Colossian heresy: 1. It appeared to set forth an impressive system of religious philosophy. 2. It was, however, a system created by the false teachers themselves ("self-imposed"), rather than being of divine origin. 3. The false teachers attempted to parade their humility. 4. This may have been done by a harsh asceticism that brutally misused the body. Paul's analysis is that such practices are worthless because they totally fail to control sinful desires. *self-imposed worship.* The false teachers themselves had created the regulations of their heretical system. They were not from God.

3:1 *then.* "Then" (or "therefore") links the doctrinal section of the letter with the practical section, just as it does in Ro 12:1; Eph 4:1; Php 4:1. *you have been raised.* Verses 1–10 set forth what has been described as the indicative and the imperative (standing and state) of the Christian. The indicative statements describe believers in Christ: They are dead (v. 3); they have been raised (v. 1); they are with Christ in heaven ("hidden with Christ," v. 3); they

you died,[x] and your life is now hidden with Christ in God. 4When
Christ, who is your[a] life,[y] appears,[z]
then you also will appear with him
in glory.[a]
5Put to death,[b] therefore, whatever belongs to your earthly nature:[c]
sexual immorality,[d] impurity, lust,
evil desires and greed,[e] which is
idolatry.[f] 6Because of these, the
wrath of God[g] is coming.[b] 7You
used to walk in these ways, in the
life you once lived.[h] 8But now you
must rid yourselves[i] of all such
things as these: anger, rage, malice,
slander,[j] and filthy language from
your lips.[k] 9Do not lie to each other,[l] since you have taken off your
old self[m] with its practices 10and
have put on the new self,[n] which is
being renewed[o] in knowledge in
the image of its Creator.[p] 11Here
there is no Greek or Jew,[q] circumcised or uncircumcised,[r] barbarian,
Scythian, slave or free,[s] but Christ
is all,[t] and is in all.
12Therefore, as God's chosen people, holy and dearly loved, clothe
yourselves[u] with compassion, kindness, humility,[v] gentleness and patience.[w] 13Bear with each other[x] and
forgive whatever grievances you
may have against one another. Forgive as the Lord forgave you.[y] 14And
over all these virtues put on love,[z]
which binds them all together in
perfect unity.[a]
15Let the peace of Christ[b] rule in
your hearts, since as members of
one body[c] you were called to
peace.[d] And be thankful. 16Let the
word of Christ[e] dwell in you richly
as you teach and admonish one another with all wisdom,[f] and as you
sing psalms,[g] hymns and spiritual
songs with gratitude in your hearts

3:1 [x]S Mk 16:19 **3:2** [w]Php 3:19,20 **3:3** [x]S Ro 6:2; 2Co 5:14 **3:4** [y]Gal 2:20 [z]1Co 1:7 [a]1Pe 1:13; 1Jn 3:2 **3:5** [b]S Ro 6:2; S Eph 4:22 [c]S Gal 5:24 [d]S 1Co 6:18 [e]Eph 5:3 [f]Gal 5:19-21; Eph 5:5 **3:6** [g]S Ro 1:18 **3:7** [h]S Eph 2:2 **3:8** [i]S Eph 4:22 [j]Eph 4:31 [k]Eph 4:29 **3:9** [l]S Eph 4:22, 25 [m]S Ro 6:6 **3:10** [n]S Ro 6:4; S 13:14 [o]Ro 12:2; S 2Co 4:16; Eph 4:23 [p]Eph 2:10 **3:11** [q]Ro 10:12; 1Co 12:13

3:11 [r]S 1Co 7:19 [s]Gal 3:28 [t]Eph 1:23 **3:12** [u]ver 10 [v]Php 2:3 [w]2Co 6:6; Gal 5:22,23; Eph 4:2 **3:13** [x]Eph 4:2 [y]Eph 4:32 **3:14** [z]1Co 13:1-13 [a]S Ro 15:5 **3:15** [b]S Jn 14:27 [c]S Ro 12:5

[a] *4* Some manuscripts *our* [b] *6* Some early manuscripts *coming on those who are disobedient*

[d]S Ro 14:19 **3:16** [e]Ro 10:17 [f]Col 1:28 [g]Ps 47:7

have "taken off the old self" (v. 9); and they have "put on the new self" (v. 10). The imperative statements indicate what believers are to do as a result: set their hearts (or minds) on things above (vv. 1–2); put to death practices that belong to their earthly nature (v. 5); and rid themselves of practices that characterized the unregenerate self (v. 8). In summary, they are called upon to become in daily experience what they are in Christ (cf. Ro 6:1–13).

3:4 *appears.* Refers to Christ's second coming (see Jn 3:2).

3:5,8 See note on Ro 1:29–31.

3:6 *wrath of God.* See notes on Zec 1:2; Ro 1:18. God is unalterably opposed to sin and will invariably make sure that it is justly punished.

3:9–10 *taken off . . . put on.* As one takes off dirty clothes and puts on clean ones, so Christians are called upon to renounce their evil ways and live in accordance with the rules of Christ's kingdom (see vv. 12–14; cf. Ro 13:12; Gal 3:27; Eph 4:22–24).

3:10 *renewed.* See 2 Co 5:17. *knowledge.* See 1:10; 2:2–3 and note on 2:3. *image of its Creator.* See note on Ge 1:26.

3:11 *barbarian.* Someone who did not speak Greek and was thought to be uncivilized. *Scythian.* Scythians were known especially for their brutality and were considered by others as little better than wild beasts. They came originally from what is today south Russia. *Christ is all, and is in all.* Christ transcends all barriers and unifies people from all cultures, races and nations. Such distinctions are no longer significant. Christ alone matters (see Gal 3:28 and note).

3:12 *God's chosen people.* Israel was called this (Dt 4:37), and so is the Christian community (1Pe 2:9; see note there). Divine election is a constant theme in Paul's letters (see note on Eph 1:4), but the Bible never teaches that it dulls human responsibility. On the contrary, as this verse shows, it is precisely because Christians have been "chosen" for eternal salvation that they must put forth every effort to live the godly life. For Paul, divine sovereignty and human responsibility go hand in hand. *clothe . . . with.* See note on Ps 109:29).

3:14 See 1Co 13:13 and note.

3:15 *peace of Christ.* The attitude of peace that Christ alone gives—in place of the attitude of bitterness and quarrelsomeness. This attitude is to "rule" (lit. "function like an umpire") in all human relationships (cf. Mt 10:34 and note). *be thankful.* See Eph 5:20 and note.

3:16 *word of Christ.* Refers especially to Christ's teaching, which in the time of the Colossians was transmitted orally. But by implication it includes the OT as well as the NT. *psalms, hymns and spiritual songs.* Some of the most important doctrines were expressed in Christian hymns preserved for us now only in Paul's letters (1:15–20; Eph 5:14; Php to God.[h] [17]And whatever you do,[i] whether in word or deed, do it all in the name of the Lord Jesus, giving thanks[j] to God the Father through him.

Rules for Christian Households

3:18–4:1pp — Eph 5:22—6:9

[18]Wives, submit to your husbands,[k] as is fitting in the Lord.

[19]Husbands, love your wives and do not be harsh with them.

[20]Children, obey your parents in everything, for this pleases the Lord.

[21]Fathers, do not embitter your children, or they will become discouraged.

[22]Slaves, obey your earthly masters in everything; and do it, not only when their eye is on you and to win their favor, but with sincerity of heart and reverence for the Lord. [23]Whatever you do, work at it with all your heart, as working for the Lord, not for men, [24]since you know that you will receive an inheritance[l] from the Lord as a reward.[m] It is the Lord Christ you are serving. [25]Anyone who does wrong will be repaid for his wrong, and there is no favoritism.[n]

4 Masters, provide your slaves with what is right and fair,[o] because you know that you also have a Master in heaven.

Further Instructions

[2]Devote yourselves to prayer,[p] being watchful and thankful. [3]And pray for us, too, that God may open a door[q] for our message, so that we may proclaim the mystery[r] of Christ, for which I am in chains.[s] [4]Pray that I may proclaim it clearly, as I should. [5]Be wise[t] in the way you act toward outsiders;[u] make the most of every opportunity.[v] [6]Let your conversation be always full of grace,[w] seasoned with salt,[x] so that you may know how to answer everyone.[y]

Final Greetings

[7]Tychicus[z] will tell you all the news about me. He is a dear brother, a faithful minister and fellow servant[a] in the Lord. [8]I am sending him to you for the express purpose that you may know about our[a] circumstances and that he may encourage your hearts.[b] [9]He is coming with Onesimus,[c] our faithful

Cross references

3:16	[g]S Ps 5:19
3:17	[h]1Co 10:31
	[i]S Eph 5:20
3:18	[k]S Eph 5:22
3:24	[l]S Ac 20:32
	[m]S Mt 16:27
3:25	[n]S Ac 10:34
4:1	[o]Lev 25:43,53
4:2	[p]S Lk 18:1
4:3	[q]S Ac 14:27
	[r]S Ro 16:25
	[s]S Ac 21:33
4:5	[t]S Eph 5:15
	[u]S Mk 4:11
	[v]Eph 5:16
4:6	[w]Eph 4:29
	[x]Mk 9:50 [y]1Pe 3:15
4:7	[z]S Ac 20:4
	[a]Eph 6:21,22;
	Col 1:7
4:8	[b]Eph 6:21,22;
	Col 2:2
4:9	[c]Phm 10

[a] 8 Some manuscripts *that he may know about your*

2:6–11; 1Ti 3:16). "Psalms" refers to the OT psalms (see Lk 20:42; 24:44; Ac 1:20; 13:33), some of which may have been set to music by the church. "Psalm" could also describe a song newly composed for Christian worship (cf. 1Co 14:26, where "hymn" is lit. "psalm" in the Greek text). A "hymn" was a song of praise, especially used in a celebration (see Mt 26:30 and note; Heb 2:12), much like the OT psalms that praised God for all that he is. A "song" recounted the acts of God and praised him for them (see Rev 5:9 and note; 15:3), much like the OT psalms that thanked God for all that he had done. See Eph 5:19 and note.

3:18—4:1 See Eph 5:22—6:9 and notes.

3:20 *in everything.* In everything not sinful (see Ac 5:29).

3:22—4:1 Paul neither condones slavery nor sanctions revolt against masters. Rather, he calls on both slaves and masters to show Christian principles in their relationship and thus to attempt to change the institution from within. The reason Paul writes more about slaves and masters than about wives, husbands, children and fathers may be that the slave Onesimus (4:9) is going along with Tychicus to deliver this Colossian letter and the letter to Philemon, Onesimus's master, who also lived in Colosse.

3:24 *inheritance.* See 1Pe 1:4; Heb 9:15 and notes.

3:25 *no favoritism.* See Ac 10:34 and note.

4:2 *Devote yourselves to prayer.* See notes on Lk 11:1; Ac 2:42; Ro 12:12; 1Th 5:17. *being watchful.* Being spiritually alert. *being . . . thankful.* See Eph 5:20 and note.

4:3 *mystery.* See notes on 1:26–27; Ro 11:25.

4:5 *outsiders.* Non-Christians (see 1Co 5:12–13; 1Th 4:12; 1Ti 3:7). *make the most of every opportunity.* See Eph 5:16 and note.

4:6 *seasoned with salt.* Salt is a preservative and is tasty. Similarly, the Christian's conversation is to be wholesome (see 3:8; Eph 4:29).

4:7 *Tychicus.* See note on Eph 6:21.

4:9–17 Onesimus (v. 9), Aristarchus (v. 10), Mark (v. 10), Epaphras (v. 12), Luke (v. 14), Demas (v. 14) and Archippus (v. 17) are mentioned in Philemon. This and dear brother, who is one of you.[d] They will tell you everything that is happening here.

[10]My fellow prisoner Aristarchus[e] sends you his greetings, as does Mark,[f] the cousin of Barnabas.[g] (You have received instructions about him; if he comes to you, welcome him.) [11]Jesus, who is called Justus, also sends greetings. These are the only Jews among my fellow workers[h] for the kingdom of God, and they have proved a comfort to me. [12]Epaphras,[i] who is one of you[j] and a servant of Christ Jesus, sends greetings. He is always wrestling in prayer for you,[k] that you may stand firm in all the will of God, mature[l] and fully assured. [13]I vouch for him

that he is working hard for you and for those at Laodicea[m] and Hierapolis. [14]Our dear friend Luke,[n] the doctor, and Demas[o] send greetings. [15]Give my greetings to the brothers at Laodicea,[p] and to Nympha and the church in her house.[q]

[16]After this letter has been read to you, see that it is also read[r] in the church of the Laodiceans and that you in turn read the letter from Laodicea.

[17]Tell Archippus:[s] "See to it that you complete the work you have received in the Lord."[t]

[18]I, Paul, write this greeting in my own hand.[u] Remember[v] my chains.[w] Grace be with you.[x]

4:9 [d]ver 12	
4:10 [e]S Ac 19:29	
[f]S Ac 12:12	
[g]S Ac 4:36	
4:11 [h]S Php 2:25	
4:12 [i]Col 1:7; Phm 23 / ver 9	
[j]S Ro 15:30	
[k]S 1Co 2:6	
4:13 [m]S Col 2:1	
4:14 [n]2Ti 4:11; Phm 24 [o]2Ti 4:10; Phm 24	
4:15 [p]S Col 2:1	
[q]S Ro 16:5	
4:16 [r]2Th 3:14; S 1Ti 4:13	
4:17 [s]Phm 2 [t]2Ti 4:5	
4:18 [u]S 1Co 16:21 [v]Heb 13:3	
[w]S Ac 21:33	
[x]1Ti 6:21; 2Ti 4:22; Tit 3:15; Heb 13:25	

---

suggests that the letters to Colosse and Philemon were written at the same time and place.

4:9 *Onesimus.* See Introduction to Philemon: Recipient, Background and Purpose.

🔲 **4:10** *Aristarchus.* A Macedonian, who is mentioned three times in Acts: 1. He was with Paul during the Ephesian riot (Ac 19:29) and therefore was known in Colosse. 2. Both he and Tychicus (Ac 20:4) were with Paul in Greece. 3. He accompanied Paul on his trip to Rome (Ac 27:2). *Mark.* The author of the second Gospel. Against Barnabas's advice, Paul refused to take Mark on the second missionary journey because Mark had "deserted" him at Pamphylia (see Ac 15:38 and note). But now—about 12 years later—the difficulties seem to have been ironed out, because Paul, both here and in Phm 24 (sent at the same time to Philemon, who was in Colosse), sends Mark's greetings. About five years later, Paul even writes that Mark "is very helpful to me in my ministry" (2Ti 4:11). See note on Ac 15:39.

4:13 *Hierapolis.* A town in Asia Minor (present-day Turkey), about 6 miles from Laodicea (see map, p. 2599) and 14 miles from Colosse. Its church may have been founded during Paul's three-year stay in Ephesus (Ac 19), but probably not by Paul himself (cf. 2:1).

🔲 **4:14** *Luke.* Wrote about Paul in the book of Acts, having often accompanied him on his travels (see note on Ac 16:10). He was with Paul in Rome during his imprisonment (Ac 28), where this

letter was written. *Demas.* A Christian worker who would later desert Paul (2Ti 4:10).

4:15 *church in her house.* For the most part, the early church had no buildings, so it usually met for worship and instruction in homes. It often centered around one family, as, e.g., Priscilla and Aquila (Ro 16:5; 1Co 16:19), Philemon (Phm 2) and Mary the mother of John (Ac 12:12).

4:16 *After this letter has been read to you.* The practice of the early church was to read Paul's letters aloud to the assembled congregation. *letter from Laodicea.* Probably not a letter by the Laodiceans. Rather, it was likely one that the Laodiceans were to lend to the Colossians—a letter that Paul had originally written to the Laodiceans. This may have been a fourth letter that Tychicus carried to this area in what is present-day Turkey, in addition to Ephesians, Colossians and Philemon. Or it could have been Paul's letter to the Ephesians—a circular letter making the rounds from Ephesus to Laodicea to Colosse (see Introduction to Ephesians: Author, Date and Place of Writing).

4:17 *Archippus.* Phm 2 calls him Paul's "fellow soldier."

4:18 Paul's custom was to dictate his letters (see Ro 16:22) and pen a few greetings himself (1Co 16:21; Gal 6:11; 2Th 3:17; Phm 19). His personal signature was the guarantee of the genuineness of the letter. *Grace.* See note on Ro 1:7. *with you.* See note on 2Co 13:14.

What Goes Into the Mind ™
Comes Out In a Life

For more life-enriching resources:
call 800-991-7747
or visit www.whatgoesintothemind.com

Want to change the world?

Think small.

You want to make a difference in the world, but there are so many needs that it can feel overwhelming. Maybe you can't change the whole world. But you can change the world for one child. When you sponsor a child through Compassion's Christ-centered, church-based program, you offer him numerous opportunities that can change his life — and his world — forever.

Through your sponsorship, a child receives:
• Educational opportunities
• Improved health care
• The chance to hear the gospel

You can also exchange letters with your child, so he can be assured of your love and encouragement.

Compassion
Releasing children from poverty
in Jesus' name

What Goes Into the Mind™
Comes Out In a Life

For more life-enriching resources:
call 800-991-7747
or visit www.whatgoesintothemind.com

$2 OFF!
Love Comes Softly

Redeem this coupon for $2 off the regular retail price.

Offer good only at the store that provided this sampler. Limit one coupon per book, one book per coupon. Coupon cannot be copied or combined with other offers or discounts.

Expiration date: September 30, 2004.

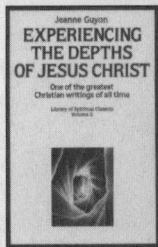

ISBN: 0764228323

$2 OFF!
Come Away My Beloved

Redeem this coupon for $2 off the regular retail price.

Offer good only at the store that provided this sampler. Limit one coupon per book, one book per coupon. Coupon cannot be copied or combined with other offers or discounts.

Expiration date: September 30, 2004.

ISBN: 1593100221

$2 OFF!
More Than a Carpenter

Redeem this coupon for $2 off the regular retail price.

Offer good only at the store that provided this sampler. Limit one coupon per book, one book per coupon. Coupon cannot be copied or combined with other offers or discounts.

Expiration date: September 30, 2004.

ISBN: 0-8423-4552-3

$2 OFF!
Experiencing the Depths of Jesus Christ

Redeem this coupon for $2 off the regular retail price.

Offer good only at the store that provided this sampler. Limit one coupon per book, one book per coupon. Coupon cannot be copied or combined with other offers or discounts.

Expiration date: September 30, 2004.

ISBN: 0-940232-00-6

Attention participating CBA Member Store: For refund of this coupon minus a handling fee, return all original coupons to CBA Sampler, P.O. Box 62000, Colorado Springs, CO 80962-2000. All coupons for this promotion must be returned in the same envelope no later than October 15, 2004. Only one refund per store will be issued for this promotion.

Coupon redeemed at:

Date:

Attention participating CBA Member Store: For refund of this coupon minus a handling fee, return all original coupons to CBA Sampler, P.O. Box 62000, Colorado Springs, CO 80962-2000. All coupons for this promotion must be returned in the same envelope no later than October 15, 2004. Only one refund per store will be issued for this promotion.

Coupon redeemed at:

Date:

Attention participating CBA Member Store: For refund of this coupon minus a handling fee, return all original coupons to CBA Sampler, P.O. Box 62000, Colorado Springs, CO 80962-2000. All coupons for this promotion must be returned in the same envelope no later than October 15, 2004. Only one refund per store will be issued for this promotion.

Coupon redeemed at:

Date:

Attention participating CBA Member Store: For refund of this coupon minus a handling fee, return all original coupons to CBA Sampler, P.O. Box 62000, Colorado Springs, CO 80962-2000. All coupons for this promotion must be returned in the same envelope no later than October 15, 2004. Only one refund per store will be issued for this promotion.

Coupon redeemed at:

Date:

Attention participating CBA Member Store: For refund of this coupon minus a handling fee, return all original coupons to CBA Sampler, P.O. Box 62000, Colorado Springs, CO 80962-2000. All coupons for this promotion must be returned in the same envelope no later than October 15, 2004. Only one refund per store will be issued for this promotion.

Coupon redeemed at:

Date:

$2 OFF!
Desiring God

Redeem this coupon for $2 off the regular retail price.

Offer good only at the store that provided this sampler. Limit one coupon per book, one book per coupon. Coupon cannot be copied or combined with other offers or discounts.

Expiration date: September 30, 2004.

ISBN: 1-59052-119-6

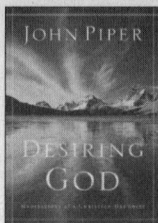

$2 OFF!
Love Must Be Tough

Redeem this coupon for $2 off the regular retail price.

Offer good only at the store that provided this sampler. Limit one coupon per book, one book per coupon. Coupon cannot be copied or combined with other offers or discounts.

Expiration date: September 30, 2004.

ISBN: 1-59052-355-5

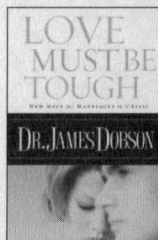

$2 OFF!
Love Not the World

Redeem this coupon for $2 off the regular retail price.

Offer good only at the store that provided this sampler. Limit one coupon per book, one book per coupon. Coupon cannot be copied or combined with other offers or discounts.

Expiration date: September 30, 2004.

ISBN: 0-87508-787-6

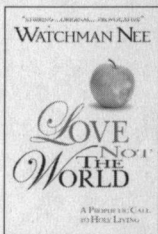

$2 OFF!
The Calvary Road

Redeem this coupon for $2 off the regular retail price.

Offer good only at the store that provided this sampler. Limit one coupon per book, one book per coupon. Coupon cannot be copied or combined with other offers or discounts.

Expiration date: September 30, 2004.

ISBN: 0-87508-788-4

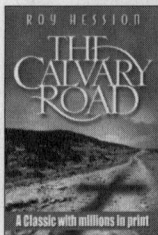

$2 OFF!
The New Evidence That Demands a Verdict

Redeem this coupon for $2 off the regular retail price.

Offer good only at the store that provided this sampler. Limit one coupon per book, one book per coupon. Coupon cannot be copied or combined with other offers or discounts.

Expiration date: September 30, 2004.

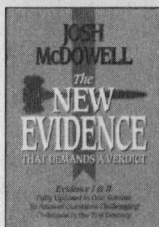

ISBN: 0785243631

$2 OFF!
Knowing God

Redeem this coupon for $2 off the regular retail price.

Offer good only at the store that provided this sampler. Limit one coupon per book, one book per coupon. Coupon cannot be copied or combined with other offers or discounts.

Expiration date: September 30, 2004. ISBNs: 0-8308-1651-8, hardcover; -1650-X, paper

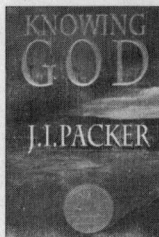

$2 OFF!
God's Best Secrets

Redeem this coupon for $2 off the regular retail price.

Offer good only at the store that provided this sampler. Limit one coupon per book, one book per coupon. Coupon cannot be copied or combined with other offers or discounts.

Expiration date: September 30, 2004.

ISBN: 0-8254-3277-4

$2 OFF!
Born Again

Redeem this coupon for $2 off the regular retail price.

Offer good only at the store that provided this sampler. Limit one coupon per book, one book per coupon. Coupon cannot be copied or combined with other offers or discounts.

Expiration date: September 30, 2004.

ISBN: 0-8007-9377-3

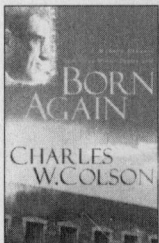

$2 OFF!
Celebration of Discipline

Redeem this coupon for $2 off the regular retail price.

Offer good only at the store that provided this sampler. Limit one coupon per book, one book per coupon. Coupon cannot be copied or combined with other offers or discounts.

Expiration date: September 30, 2004.

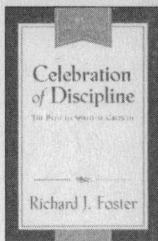

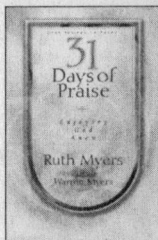

ISBN: 60628391

$2 OFF!
Practicing His Presence

Redeem this coupon for $2 off the regular retail price.

Offer good only at the store that provided this sampler. Limit one coupon per book, one book per coupon. Coupon cannot be copied or combined with other offers or discounts.

Expiration date: September 30, 2004.

ISBN: 0-940232-01-4

$2 OFF!
Shadow of the Almighty

Redeem this coupon for $2 off the regular retail price.

Offer good only at the store that provided this sampler. Limit one coupon per book, one book per coupon. Coupon cannot be copied or combined with other offers or discounts.

Expiration date: September 30, 2004.

ISBN: 006062213X

$2 OFF!
31 Days of Praise

Redeem this coupon for $2 off the regular retail price.

Offer good only at the store that provided this sampler. Limit one coupon per book, one book per coupon. Coupon cannot be copied or combined with other offers or discounts.

Expiration date: September 30, 2004.

ISBN: 1-57673-875-2

$2 OFF!

The Pursuit of God

Redeem this coupon for $2 off the regular retail price.

Offer good only at the store that provided this sampler. Limit one coupon per book, one book per coupon. Coupon cannot be copied or combined with other offers or discounts.

Expiration date: September 30, 2004.

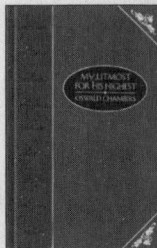

ISBN: 0875093663

$2 OFF!

Mountain Breezes

Redeem this coupon for $2 off the regular retail price.

Offer good only at the store that provided this sampler. Limit one coupon per book, one book per coupon. Coupon cannot be copied or combined with other offers or discounts.

Expiration date: September 30, 2004. ISBNs: 0-87508-790-6, hardcover; -789-2, paper

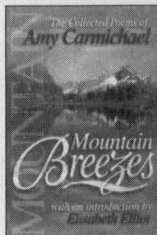

$2 OFF!

The Pilgrim's Progress

Redeem this coupon for $2 off the regular retail price.

Offer good only at the store that provided this sampler. Limit one coupon per book, one book per coupon. Coupon cannot be copied or combined with other offers or discounts.

Expiration date: September 30, 2004.

ISBN: 0-941478-02-5

$2 OFF!

My Utmost for His Highest

Redeem this coupon for $2 off the regular retail price.

Offer good only at the store that provided this sampler. Limit one coupon per book, one book per coupon. Coupon cannot be copied or combined with other offers or discounts.

Expiration date: September 30, 2004.

ISBN: 1-57748-914-4

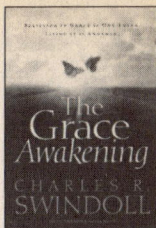

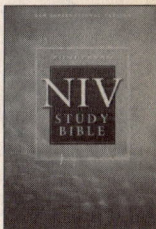

WHAT GOES INTO THE MIND™
COMES OUT IN A LIFE

For more life-enriching resources:
call 800-991-7747
or visit www.whatgoesintothemind.com